What is a Minister?

What is a Minister?

Edited by Esther Shreeve
and Philip Luscombe

EPWORTH PRESS

British Library Cataloguing in Publication data

A catalogue record for this book is available
from the British Library

07162 0559 9

First published in 2002
by Epworth Press
20 Ivatt way
Peterborough, PE3 7PG

Typeset by Regent Typesetting, London
and printed in Great Britain by Biddles Ltd,
www.biddles.co.uk

Contents

Acknowledgements

We would like to thank the many people without whose support this book would never have seen the light of day. Our colleagues in the Cambridge Theological Federation and fellow members of the Methodist Tutors' Meeting wanted it to happen. The Formation in Ministry team, and especially Ken Howcroft, have been consistently enthusiastic and helpful; their budget paid for the Consultation in Cambridge, which was then most ably facilitated by the support staff at Wesley House and the East Anglian Ministerial Training Course. Gerald Burt at the Epworth Press has been unflagging in his willingness to advise. We have benefited enormously from his wisdom and graciousness. Janice Pettipher, one of our students, came to the rescue at the end (when time was fast running out!) to help with proof-reading. Finally and most importantly, our families, Laurel and Ben; Chris, Sarah and Nathan, have been most patient and encouraging, putting up with extra work being slotted into already very crowded schedules without a grumble. This is a book about one part of the complex pattern of ministry, and we would like to dedicate it to everyone who is engaged in Christ's ministry, in whatever form that may take.

Esther Shreeve
Philip Luscombe
Cambridge, Advent 2001

The Contributors

Clifford Bellamy is a full-time District Judge at the Leeds Combined Court Centre, a post he has held since 1995. He is also a Methodist minister, having been ordained in 2001. As a Methodist minister he is in a sector appointment at Leeds Methodist Mission, though he is stationed in his home circuit in Chesterfield. He is married to Christine and has two sons, Christopher and Jonathan.

Richard Clutterbuck has been Principal of the West of England Ministerial Training Course since 1995. After ministerial training at the Queen's College, Birmingham, and the Irish School of Ecumenics, he spent three years as a tutor at Sia'atoutai Theological College, Tonga. Since then he has served in two north London circuits and completed a doctorate on the development of Christian doctrine. Richard Clutterbuck is married to Diane, also a Methodist presbyter, and they live in Gloucester with their two daughters.

Leslie Griffiths was a lecturer in Medieval English before training for the Methodist ministry at Wesley House, Cambridge. He spent much of the 1970s as a minister in Haiti. Since 1996 he has been superintendent minister at Wesley's Chapel. In 1994–95 he was President of the Methodist Conference. He has been a member of various Committees reflecting his interest in higher education, broadcasting and ecumenical relations. He broadcasts regularly on 'Thought for the Day' and *The Daily Service* and writes for *The Methodist Recorder* and *The Tablet*. He has published four books. He is married to Margaret and they have three children.

Kenneth Howcroft is a Methodist minister, and is currently serving as Secretary for Presbyteral Ministry and Leader of the Formation in Ministry Office in the connexional team. Having read Classics and taught for six years, he trained for the Methodist ministry at Wesley House, Cambridge, whilst completing an MPhil in New Testament Studies. He was stationed at the West London Mission at Hinde Street and served as the Ecumenical Lecturer at Lincoln Theological College. He was the main author of the *Making of Ministry* report in 1996, and has helped steer through the new patterns of ministerial training in Methodism which have resulted from it.

Sue Jackson grew up in Salford. After completing a Psychology degree she worked as a teacher in a school for children with severe learning difficulties and then as a social worker with young adults moving into 'care in the community'. Her diaconal training included taking a BD. She then married an atheist and moved into circuit working on a council over-spill estate helping set up a church-related community project. Currently she is Secretary for Continuing Development in Ministry at Methodist Church House and an Associate Warden for the Methodist Diaconal Order.

Jane Leach is a presbyter currently serving as Senior Tutor and Director of Pastoral Studies at Wesley House in Cambridge. She has a PhD in pastoral theology which looks at the construction and maintenance of Christian identity in plural culture, and she teaches pastoral theology on the Anglia Polytechnic University MA course as well as within the Cambridge Theological Federation. For the five years prior to this appointment she served in the Fenland Methodist Circuit, having pastoral charge of four rural churches.

Philip Luscombe is a presbyter and Principal of Wesley House in Cambridge. Before studying theology his training was as a physicist. He worked for 15 years as a Methodist circuit minister in London and the north-east, before becoming Director of the

Wesley Study Centre in Durham. He is the author of *Ground-work of Science and Religion* (Epworth Press, 2000) and is married to Laurel; they have one son, Benjamin.

Clive Marsh is husband to Jill, a Methodist minister, and father to Philip and Hannah. He is also Secretary of the Faith and Order Committee of the Methodist Church and a local preacher. He taught Christian theology for 11 years. He has written widely on Christology, the historical Jesus, and theology and the arts. He co-wrote *Jesus and the Gospels* (Continuum, 1999) with Steve Moyise and co-edited *Methodism and the Future* (Cassell, 1999) with Jane Craske. His most recent book is *Christianity in a Post-Atheist Age* (SCM, 2002).

Esther Shreeve is Director of Studies for the East Anglian Ministerial Training Course. She is a church historian and Methodist local preacher, married to Chris, a Methodist presbyter. Much of her career has been concerned with adult Christian education and ministerial training, and she has a keen interest in making theological education accessible and relevant for the people of God.

Andrew Todd is a Residentiary Canon of St Edmundsbury Cathedral and Continuing Ministerial Education Officer for the Diocese of St Edmundsbury and Ipswich. Until July 2001 he was Vice-Principal and Director of Studies for the East Anglian Ministerial Training Course. He is a former president of the Cambridge Theological Federation. Andrew's interests include the theology and practice of ministry, practical hermeneutics (and especially the relationship between biblical studies and ministry). With Michael West and Graham Noble, he wrote *Living Theology* (DLT, 1999).

Preface

The origins of this book were in a meeting of those teaching theology and involved in ministerial training for the British Methodist Church. When we began to ask the question, 'What is a minister or presbyter within the Methodist Church?' we received a range of responses from 'Do tell me if you find out' to 'The answer is obvious: don't talk about the question, simply get outside and minister to people.' The overwhelming response, however, was to acknowledge the importance of the question for the Church, and to wish the enterprise well. A consultation with the title 'What is a presbyter?' took place at Wesley House in Cambridge in the autumn of 2001. Many of the issues raised at Wesley House are the subject of lively debate within the Church. The Methodist Church has to make a number of decisions in the next few years about the future shape of its ordained ministry. So we have decided to publish the work of the consultation more or less as it was delivered, as an immediate contribution to the Methodist and wider debates.

The debate on the nature of ministry spreads right across the Christian Church. For some branches of the Church the pressing issue may be whether priests are permitted to marry, whether women can be priests, or the relation of sexuality to fitness for ministry. Other groups debate the place and style of leadership and authority, or the appropriate person to preside at or celebrate the sacrament of Holy Communion. Underlying many of the individual questions is a deep concern about the nature of ministry and ordained ministry as a whole. How do patterns inherited from previous generations, which may or may not be sanctioned by Scripture, relate to a society suspicious of tradition and all forms of authority?   *only one!*

We did not set out by asking each contributor to answer the same fundamental question on the nature of ministry. Instead we asked a group of people – experienced circuit ministers, teachers of theology, a lay theologian, an Anglican priest, a Methodist deacon – to address particular topics relating to the question of what a minister is. Some of the resultant chapters tackle the main question head on; others help to build up a broader picture. There are some obvious gaps. The relation of our understanding of the Church to our understanding of ministry is not addressed directly. The ministry of the bishop is only referred to in passing by one or two of the contributors, although it is currently the focus of intense argument within British Methodism. Equally there is no discussion of the theology of the ordination service itself, although the emphases of the *Methodist Worship Book* plainly underlie many of the chapters. Primarily this book is about ministry as it is experienced day by day within the Methodist Church at the start of the twenty-first century.

Is it really a little glass look?

This book attempts to provide a contribution to the larger ecumenical debate by being unapologetically Methodist. By coincidence a book of Anglican essays, *Priests in a People's Church*,[1] will be published a few months before our collection. We asked one Anglican to contribute to our consultation in order to check our perceptions and to earth our debate in the context of the wider Church, but essentially we seek to be ecumenical by being Methodist. This is how important facets of the debate appear to a reasonably representative group of Methodists. We hope that others will take up the dialogue to help us to learn how our particular concerns belong within the whole ecumenical debate.

Introduction

ESTHER SHREEVE and PHILIP LUSCOMBE

This book is about expectations. Readers will bring their own hopes or expectations to the book, trusting it may answer the question, 'What is a minister?' Perhaps it will, but it is also likely to raise more questions than it attempts to answer. The consultation which set the ball rolling never aimed to provide a definitive answer, but to give the question a thorough airing so that some, at least, of the issues would be brought out into the open. Ministers, their families and friends, circuit and church stewards, those working with ministers both within and outside the Church, and those exploring their vocation – all need to know if their expectations of what it means to be a minister are reasonable, realistic, and in line with the official statements of the Methodist Church.

Expectations can be both an inspiration and a burden. What are the expectations Methodist ministers have of themselves? There is the traditional picture of a circuit minister, which may still hold some sway, of God's servant starting work every morning at half past eight, having already spent an hour or so in Bible study and prayer. The first third of the working day would be spent preparing services and sermons, and talks for the Women's Fellowship. After lunch, the afternoon would be devoted to visiting, or leading a fellowship group; home for tea, and then out again to chair a church council, lead a Bible study group, or prepare a couple for their wedding. In between times, school assemblies, meetings of the local Churches Together group, clergy fraternals, district meetings, and the pastoral care group of

Why not Say Some At this could be Exciting ad with a bit A imagination fulfilling.

the British Legion would have to be fitted in. Of course, should a pastoral emergency arise then everything would be dropped, and the minister would be there for people in acute distress, offering an embodiment of a spiritual presence and words of hope and comfort. Presiding at the Lord's Supper at least once a month in each church, and offering Communion to the sick and house-bound would be like a golden thread running through the whole range of activities, giving a fixed point of reference and a shape to ministry which minister and congregation alike would be able to sense, if not articulate. The context in which the minister was working and living would be ideally one of a happy marriage to a supportive spouse with children who made few, if any, demands, and the whole family contributing a huge amount to the life of their local church and community.

The expectations which people within the church have of their minister may well follow this traditional pattern, even if a few adjustments may have been made as a concession to life in the twenty-first century. Most members of congregations think they know what their minister should be doing. The interesting thing is that they may well discover that they do not have the same view as the person who sits in the pew behind them every Sunday. Some may believe that the minister should be there primarily for the church or circuit which, after all, pays the ministerial stipend. If it is a multi-church situation, where the minister has pastoral charge of several chapels, there could well be conflicting expectations about where he or she should spend their time. Should the minister concentrate on the smaller, or struggling congregations, helping them to catch a vision, or should she (or he) be a regular presence in the big, growing church, where new people are already coming in, and need nurture and encouragement? Others may argue passionately that the church should, as a general rule, be able to look after its own folk, and that the minister should be working outside the confines of the cosy club, and spending time in school, hospital, prison and the community at large.

This is where the whole question of 'maintenance ministry or mission' comes into play. But it is not a simple dichotomy. We

what does that mean?

Here we go Little deal Sanisfyation.

why? with what right?

cannot take it for granted that everyone who comes to church on a Sunday understands the basics of the Christian faith, particularly as we have now experienced two generations where Sunday School attendance simply has not been an important feature in our society. The mission field is both within and outside our churches. It is bigger than it has ever been, yet the numbers of clergy, and committed church members, are smaller. Thus the demands made of ministers are great, and it is up to the individual to pick a way through the tangled web of needs to be met, responsibilities to be fulfilled, and duties to be carried out.

Those outside the church have another set of expectations – which are, perhaps, more straightforward than those the ministers and churchgoers have. The minister should be there for them when needed – usually at a time of crisis, but also for the rites of passage, official functions, or simply a leisurely chat. Yet it is true that these expectations are not formulated as demands – often the outsider is well aware how busy a minister may be, and apologizes for taking up precious time. Thus we get the story of the minister, who was also a hospital chaplain, turning up late for a church meeting because he had asked a member of staff how she was. He got the whole nine yards as her marriage was breaking up, and had to make an on-the-spot decision to stay and listen, or dash off to his meeting.

Both churchgoers and outsiders could well be astonished by the many and varied models of ministry which are a feature of the Methodist Church today. Unless their circuit actually can boast of having one, they may not know what a Minister in Local Appointment is. For those in this situation, a brief description will have to suffice: MLAs are ministers who have been through the same training and candidating procedures as itinerant ministers, but who have chosen to stay at home, usually continuing with their jobs, and who offer whatever time they can to ministry – which may be in a local circuit, or may take the form of chaplaincy work or some other specialized form of ministry. Usually they receive no remuneration apart from expenses. Then we have Sector Ministers, who carry on working full-time at their job, and exercise their ministry in the workplace.

Definitions can become blurred, as we see, for example, in the case of MLAs who are part-time teachers, but may also have pastoral charge of a church. They often exercise their ministry in school as well as the local circuit.

So, what is a minister? What are our expectations of those who are ordained to authorized ministry in the Methodist Church? Leslie Griffiths sets the ball rolling with a circuit minister's perspective on the subject. He asks whether ministry is in danger of becoming a profession rather than a vocation, a question more often found on the lips of those dissatisfied with their minister! In the context of so many different models of ordained ministry now visible, this is a vital issue to air. Jane Leach offers another view from a similar perspective. She talks of the importance of working out any definition in dialogue with the laity, the diaconate, and ecumenically. For her, 'embodiment' is crucial, a very human way of looking at the representative aspect of ordained ministry. Her vision of 'minding the gap' is of the minister bridging the gulf between the now and the not yet; our lives today, and the fulfilment of God's Kingdom on earth.

Where the minister may be found is what concerns Philip Luscombe, who speaks of our Methodist traditions, the tensions between being a minister in a circuit or in secular employment, and the relationship with the Connexion (a Methodist term for the structure which holds all of our Methodist individuals, churches, and institutions together), which the circuit minister has to carry and work with. He asks whether the itinerant model of ministry should be made redundant, or whether a new, reinvigorated style of itinerancy can be discovered, which serves God's mission.

Clifford Bellamy's work on sector ministry develops this. He rehearses the background to the introduction of this category of minister, and laments the fact that many, particularly at grass-roots level, still cannot accept an ordained minister who does not have pastoral charge. He looks carefully at the key reports and statements of the Methodist Church on ordination over the last 40 years, and points out that sector ministry is very much in line with the theology contained within them. The question of mission and/or maintenance ministry is raised again, with sector ministers having a positive part to play, both active in mission themselves and supporting others who are involved in mission and outreach work. He paints a picture of the sector minister as a 'bridge' person, someone who must be firmly supported by the church (or circuit), but also by the people of God in the sector where he or she is working. *What if laity then "can't then do whatever is, does?*

Richard Clutterbuck's approach appears to be in complete contrast to this. His chapter has a strong eucharistic emphasis, which is echoed by several others, who agree that presiding at Communion is a fundamental part of what an ordained minister does, grounded both in theological interpretation and pastoral practice. He puts presidency at the Eucharist in a much broader context of exercising oversight in several spheres, with presidency at the Lord's Table being seen as the most complete expression of the ministerial role. He quotes Schillebeeckx writing about the Church as 'the womb of ministry'.[1]

Esther Shreeve writes as a lay person concerned with the concept of collaborative ministry. In the context of the ministry of the whole people of God, she explores the responsibility of the Church as a corporate community, and the presbyter as the person with both the authority and the responsibility of oversight to discern and encourage the vocation of individual members. The Church's preoccupation with 'recognized' ministry is commented upon with reference to the way in which the Methodist Church sometimes authorizes lay people to preside at Communion.

Andrew Todd, an Anglican theologian, describes the way the Church of England has come to realize that the parish church and the local community are not identical, and how this has challenged the way Anglicans are thinking about ministry. A shift in the way apostolicity is viewed and a move towards Trinitarian rather than Christological models of ministry have led to a more mission-oriented view of ministry, which recognizes the importance of being in relationship with both people and God. He talks of the Church being the instrument by which the Kingdom of God is realized in the world, very much along

similar lines to Schillebeeckx's picture, quoted by Richard
Clutterbuck. He concludes, however, that the norm is still a
tendency to 'churchy' ministry (i.e. ministry to the Church),
rather than the ministry of the Church.

ugh!

Clive Marsh moves the discussion on to an exploration of the
tension between Church and Kingdom, basing his approach on a
Christocentric theology and an appreciation of our Reformation
heritage. His plea is that the time has come to let presbyters be
presbyters, in effect limiting their role, which will mean revitalis-
ing and refocusing both the diaconate and the laity. Ministers, he
argues, need to be rooted in, and managing, the religious communities they serve, as theologians, local guardians of the
Christian tradition, leaders of worship, and presidents at the
Eucharist.

Trinitarian theology is a strand which runs through the whole
discussion, and Deacon Sue Jackson starts with a description of
Rublev's icon of the Trinity, emphasizing the open circle portrayed there. Her careful exploration of the diaconate is most
welcome, and timely. Deacons stand on the threshold between
two places, the Church and the world. She echoes Clive Marsh's
plea to be focused, but adds flexibility to the specification. The
religious order aspect of the diaconate is also examined, raising
again the question as to whether Methodism is, in itself, a
religious order. *It is Not.*

Ken Howcroft firmly puts the question of the identity of
the presbyteral minister into the context of the Church and the
ministry of all people. We must consider the ministry of the
presbyter alongside that of lay people, deacons and bishops. He
makes a new attempt to bind together the language of the 1932
Deed of Union with that of representation and focusing from the
1974 report on 'Ordination' using insights from our ecumenical
partners. He also reminds us that the '*laos*' is in fact the whole
people of God; we cannot set the laity and the ordained over
against one another. His chapter is firmly rooted in the language
of *Our Calling*, Methodism's recent attempt to write a simple
and self-explanatory 'mission statement'.[2]

Already, it will be apparent that several common threads run through the discussions. The recent understanding of Trinitarian theology as relational means that the ordained minister's relationships to God, to the Church, and to individuals become a critical concern; the importance of presiding at the Lord's Supper, as well as leading congregations in living out the eucharistic life, is another recurring theme. 'Minding the gap', with its multi-faceted implications, the minister as a bridge, and the deacon as someone on the threshold between the Church and the world, are all worthy of more discussion. As you read, you will become aware of other questions: vocation (is this for life?), representation, mission, authority, oversight and ecumenical implications. These are explicit. Less obvious, but germane to the subject, and raised in the discussions after each paper, are gender issues, models of leadership, and tensions between corporate and individual responsibilities. Fundamental to the whole debate is 'What is the Church?' and 'Where does the minister fit in to the whole picture?' Keep these questions in mind as you read; we hope that by the time you get to the end, you will be in a position to attempt to find some answers. That is the aim of this book – to provide a basis for debate and more creative thought. This is just the beginning!

What is a Presbyter?

LESLIE GRIFFITHS

Let us begin at the beginning. A direct question needs an equally direct answer. So, seeking to provide one, I have gone straight to the appropriate section of the Deed of Union. Let the oracle speak:

*The oracle was
GS Finsley :- 1908 .*

> Christ's ministers in the church are stewards in the household of God and shepherds of his flock. Some are called and ordained to this sole occupation and have a principal and directing part in these great duties but they hold no priesthood differing in kind from that which is common to all the Lord's people and they have no exclusive title to the preaching of the gospel or the care of souls. These ministries are shared with them by others to whom also the Spirit divides his gifts severally as he wills.
>
> It is the universal conviction of the Methodist people that the office of the Christian ministry depends upon the call of God who bestows the gifts of the Spirit the grace and the fruit which indicate those whom He has chosen.[1]

And that is that. In its anxiety to stress the characteristics of the 'priesthood of all believers', this section uses the words 'minister' and 'ministries' in a muddled way. Everyone, it states, is a *minister* and yet those whose call is recognized and validated are set aside through ordination to be (that word again) *ministers*. The tasks of pastoral care and preaching the word belong to everyone within the household of faith yet some, set apart by dint

Perhaps a little explanation of what the Deed of union was is needed for the uninitiated.

of their vocation and ordination, play a principal and directing part in these occupations. Clearly, ordained ministry is considered here to be an activity (a way of life) committed to a small part of the church by the general membership. The emphasis is always upon the fact that such ministers are no different in kind, nor do their functions differ, from the nature and work of the whole membership. In all this, of course, the word 'presbyter' never appears. Within Methodist parlance, it's a parvenu, an upstart, a somewhat angular and brash new arrival within a vocabulary that has made elbow room for it under the pressure of contemporary ecumenical dialogue and certain developments within our own Methodist Church. *It was earlier — actual fact.*

Thus spake J. Scott Lidgett *et al.* in 1932. And now we must give our attention to what we did not then (but do now) call presbyteral ministry, a matter which, as a Church, we have never really got sorted out. I want to suggest that developments since the Second World War have hardly helped.

? No When I began my ministry, there were 'lay pastors' in the land; they wore clerical dress and, to the untrained eye, they seemed to be both lay *and* ordained, ministerial hermaphrodites. The fact that they were not ordained simply added to the mystery. No *They were much earlier.* doubt, this was a category of ministry created to help with shortages during and after the war, a pragmatic response to need. With the return of normality, they were eventually phased out. But soon a bewildering range of developments began to occur. Sector Ministers appeared, causing untold agonies about what it meant to be ordained whilst working for a secular employer. The case of Jack Burton, bus driver both *débonnaire* and *extraordinaire*, had raised all these questions in a particularly acute way. He was eventually given 'permission to serve in other appointments', the only way of dealing with him in those days. But his case set the ball rolling and sector ministry ensued. Ministers in Local Appointment followed a generation later and this category contained an implicit challenge to the notion of itinerancy. Women were ordained from the 1970s, a most welcome and long overdue development which did, however, bring a few unexpected questions in its wake: how to station

'ministerial couples' for example. Nigel Collinson gave utterance to his dream of 'a pastor in every church' and this became a rallying cry for an understanding of church that seemed to be denied by our circuit system where ministers' time and energy became ever more stretched and divided as their numbers decreased. And then came talk of Ministers with District Licence who would be neither 'in full connexion' nor itinerant and who, if I understood the proposal properly, would be able to cease to be ministers as quickly as they acquired that status.

All these developments have been within the sphere of presbyteral ministry. Meanwhile, the Deaconess Order was fading away to be replaced (hastily in the view of some) by a Diaconal Order of Ministry whose members may (or may not) be given dispensation to administer Holy Communion and who, functionally at least, are often indistinguishable from presbyters. Lay Workers, a title which began by describing an ephemeral category of church worker, task-specific and definitely a short-term expedient, have become more and more 'full blown', with pension rights, renewable contracts, training and study entitlements and career paths very much part of their picture. Once more, the work done by lay workers can look very much like that undertaken by presbyters (and it certainly evokes memories of those lay pastors with which this Cook's Tour of recent developments in ministry began). Indeed, a lay worker's position is often created to fill the gap left by the withdrawal of a presbyter. When compounded by a dispensation to administer the sacrament, such posts make for even greater confusion.

Throughout all these developments in the ranks of 'paid staff', we have been reminding ourselves of 'The Ministry of the Whole People of God' (a title more chic than 'the priesthood of all believers'). Nothing done by our mercenaries should marginalize or diminish the contribution of the 'ordinary' church membership (even though we have signally been unable to agree exactly what we mean these days by 'membership'. To address *that* one, we would need another volume entitled 'What is a Member?'). To cap everything, the recently introduced 'Foundation Training' seeks to offer training and formation to anyone in the

Church, envisaging theologically literate circuit stewards, for example, *just as much as the formation of those we used to call 'ministers'*.

In all these developments, the nature and understanding of presbyteral ministry has been profoundly modified, most often by silent erosion and certainly without much informed comment. Its traditional shape and character has died (is dying) the death of a thousand cuts. Those of us who have lived through this period might be forgiven if sometimes we feel as if someone has been sawing through the branch of the tree we happen to be sitting on. This volume is a welcome (if belated) attempt to take stock of a confusing situation. I suspect it will be like taking a snapshot of melting butter.

Meanwhile, if we lift our heads above the parapet for a moment and take stock of the way the 'world' sees our presbyteral ministry, everything will become even more alarming. In my years at Wesley House, our Wednesday sermon class had a very strictly enforced timing. It all had to be out of the way by 9.30 p.m. to allow Gordon and Marjorie Rupp their weekly opportunity to watch *All Gas and Gaiters*. Derek Nimmo's portrayal of the ineffectual clergyman was brilliant. It challenged a revered stereotype and poked fun at a figure previously immune from such treatment. *Father Ted*, *The Vicar of Dibley* and even the current *Private Eye* satire which casts Tony Blair in the guise of the Vicar of Albion have in their own ways continued this trend.

The elopement of the Bishop of Argyll and the Moonie marriage of the Archbishop of Malingo have filled many pages of newsprint. The media have always loved a 'vicar runs away with choirmistress' story, but the recent flurry of child abuse revelations and the spate of lawsuits which threatens to bankrupt the Roman Catholic Church in the USA and Canada have taken such material into unthinkable realms. Add in the continued numerical decline of mainstream denominations, and the secular world finds less and less reason to consult, respect or maintain an awareness of the Church and its appointed officers. In all this, the presbyteral role has come to count for peanuts.

If then, both from within and without the Church, those who

are theologically the representative people, the recognizable faces of organized Christianity, are more and more tangential to the fabric both of the churches they serve and also of civil society, it is not difficult to agree that a crisis of identity, a confusion of purpose and a lack of direction might all typify the times we are living in. It certainly makes the question being addressed within these pages an urgent one.

To begin my attempt to define (or rediscover) the essential ontological and functional identity of the presbyter, I would like to slip back into the fourteenth century and to one of our culture's greatest figures. Geoffrey Chaucer lived at a time when there was an array of ministries within the Church at least as kaleidoscopic as in our own day. The Prologue to his *Canterbury Tales* introduces us to a number of ecclesiastical office holders. We meet a nun, a monk, a friar, a cleric, a few priests, a summoner, a pardoner, and (of course) a parson – all travelling as members of a riotous and bawdy band of pilgrims going off to a Canterbury that sounds more interesting then than now. Listen hard:

> A holy-minded man of good renown
> There was, and poor, the *Parson* to a town,
> Yet he was rich in holy thought and work.
> He also was a learned man, a clerk,
> Who truly knew Christ's gospel and would preach it
> Devoutly to parishioners, and teach it.
> Benign and wonderfully diligent,
> And patient when adversity was sent
> (For so he proved in much adversity)
> He hated cursing to extort a fee,
> Nay rather he preferred beyond a doubt
> Giving to poor parishioners round about
> Both from church offerings and his property;
> He could in little find sufficiency.
> Wide was his parish, with houses far asunder,
> Yet he neglected not in rain or thunder,
> In sickness or in grief, to pay a call

On the remotest, whether great or small,
Upon his feet, and in his hand a stave.
This noble example to his sheep he gave
That first he wrought, and afterwards he taught;
And it was from the Gospel he had caught
Those words, and he would add this figure too,
That if gold rust, what then will iron do?
For if a priest be foul in whom we trust
No wonder that a common man would rust;
And shame it is to see – let priests take stock –
A shitten shepherd and a snowy flock.
The true example that a priest should give
Is one of cleanness, how the sheep should live.
He did not set his benefice to hire
And leave his sheep encumbered in the mire
Or run to London to earn easy bread
By singing masses for the wealthy dead,
Or find some Brotherhood and get enrolled.
He stayed at home and watched over his fold
So that no wolf should make the sheep miscarry.
He was a shepherd and no mercenary.
Holy and virtuous he was, but then
Never contemptuous of sinful men,
Never disdainful, never too proud or fine,
But was discreet in teaching and benign.
His business was to show a fair behaviour
And draw men thus to Heaven and their Saviour,
Unless indeed a man were obstinate:
And such, whether of high or low estate,
He put to sharp rebuke, to say the least.
I think there never was a better priest.
He sought no pomp or glory in his dealing,
No scrupulosity had spiced his feelings.
Christ and his twelve apostles and their lore
He taught, but followed it himself before. [2]

Wouldn't the Stationing Committee love to have a few such

people at its disposal? But what springs out of this lovely pen portrait, a jewel in the crown of one of our literature's finest works, is a downright respect for the office of presbyter. This lovely man, seen as one of a bunch of people who are all caught up in 'ministry' of one kind or another, whether selling pardons or begging for money, living the life of Riley or exploring different orientations and lifestyles, this 'presbyter', stands out like a pikestaff. His commitment to his people is obvious. So too is his patent goodness; we catch sight of his roles as teacher, preacher and pastor; his approach to his work can never be called mercenary; and all these admirable qualities are gathered within a man who clearly understands the need to set an appropriate example to his parishioners. For him, the priestly role was more a matter of vocation than profession, more a life to live than a job to perform.

I suggest that the model offered here by Geoffrey Chaucer would once (and not too long ago at that) have rung bells within any discussion of presbyteral ministry undertaken by a Methodist group. I have the feeling that this model is now much harder to define and defend within a Church that has been affected by the secular discussion of employment (and, indeed, human) rights. What is more, one of the unexpected consequences of taking older men and women into our ministry is that they often come with baggage they learned to carry in their previous working lives. Often they want to work to a contract, they want to spell out a specific length for their working day/week, they seek to define and quantify their rights and entitlements, they import managerial styles and approaches to work, and so on. And those of us whose path into ministry began in our (relative) youth, and who are still in touch with an ethos that pre-dates many of these later developments, hear ourselves caricatured again and again as 'workaholics', 'doormats', 'out of touch', or 'inefficient'.

I know well enough, of course, that I am not putting forward a fashionable point of view and anyone more scholarly than I will have all the tools they need to discount and dismiss substantial parts of this analysis of mine as being subjective and anecdotal. I readily admit that I cannot support my opinions

EVEn clauea was a bit Nealiske!!

with oodles of statistical material gathered from intricate questionnaires sent out to an adequate sample of practitioners, the results then being fed through a computer. But I would urge anyone who reads these lines, the efforts of one whose only labour has been that of a circuit minister and who has certainly reflected long and hard upon his endeavours and experience (to say nothing of the Church around him), not merely to smile politely at my musings while awaiting the earliest opportunity to get the discussion back onto an even, scholarly, dispassionate keel. The issues which spring from all my ruminating are fundamental to the question being addressed by this little volume. The notion of a presbyteral ministry that functions as vocation rather than profession and a model of ministry rooted in the idea of 'representativeness' that is at the heart of the ordination service, has been severely eroded by changing patterns and perceptions. In all this, in our search for greater variety, equal opportunity, pragmatic responses to the organizational and managerial needs of the Church, is it not time to ask just how much we have lost? Do we regret losing it? And, if we do, is any of it recoverable? Or desirable?

It may be thought odd that in my attempts to define the role and identity of a presbyter in the twenty-first century, I have quoted (at such length) a piece of poetry from the fourteenth. I did so because it seemed a clear enough picture for all of us to understand and because it raises sharply all the issues we are likely to discuss in these pages. For those who would like something a tad more modern I can certainly oblige with two examples. ⌐ɑ ᴡʜɑᴛ ᵗ Sᴏᴍᴇᴡʜɑᵗ (ᴏᴇᴅ/

First of all, an illustration that throws a somewhat negative light on the ministerial office but one which, nevertheless, might allow us to focus on the identity and role of those who hold it. Almost 50 years ago, R. S. Thomas wrote a short verse drama for the BBC which he called 'The Minister'. Two short extracts show opposing points of view about the qualities and standing of the eponymous hero of the piece. The sullen and malign lay people who meet to choose their next incumbent have some clear criteria to work with:

The chose their pastors as they chose their horses
For hard work. But the last one died
Sooner than they expected; nothing sinister,
You understand, but just the natural
Breaking of the heart beneath a load
Unfit for horses. 'Ay, he's a good 'un,'
Job Davies had said; and Job was a master
Hand at choosing a nag or a pastor.
And Job was right, but he forgot,
They all forgot, that even a pastor
Is a man first and a minister after,
Although he wears the sober armour
Of God, and wields the fiery tongue
Of God, and listens to the voice
Of God, the voice no others listen to.[3]

That is the way these grim men approach the task of choosing their minister. They see him as bringing God's word to them. But they also see very clearly that he is to be kept firmly under their control. Even as they idealized the virtues they were looking for, they were never going to allow him to suffer any illusion of exactly who was in charge. It was not going to be the minister himself. And God did not get into the frame. They, and they alone, his paymasters, would always have the last word. The minister, once appointed, would have a steep learning curve. He would have to fit their expectations. None of his imaginative or even worthy initiatives win their approval or support. For all that, he soon finds he has a power over his people, the power of knowledge. Here is one of his soliloquies:

I was the chapel pastor, the abrupt shadow
Staining the neutral fields, troubling the men
Who grew there with my glib, dutiful praise
Of a fool's world; a man ordained for ever
To pick his way along the grass-strewn wall
Dividing tact from truth.
                              I knew it all,

Although I never pried, I knew it all.
I knew why Buddig was away from chapel.
I knew that Pritchard, the *Fron*, watered his milk.
I knew who put the ferret with the fowls
In Pugh's hen-house. I knew and pretended I didn't.
And they knew that I knew and pretended I didn't.
They listened to me preaching the unique gospel
Of love; but our eyes never met. And outside
The blood of God darkened the evening sky.[4]

This was the Free Church notion of ministry I grew up with in Wales. Congregational, local, controlled. Its limitations are well enough portrayed in Richard Llewellyn's *How Green was my Valley*. Mercifully, our connexionalism saves us from some of these dynamics. But these verses should allow us to renew our commitment to a presbyteral office which, while representative and accountable, is not at the mercy of local (financial) control. R. S. Thomas's minister is unable to exercise his prophetic role; he is disempowered from his charge to 'admonish' the flock; he is, by the nature of his position, a mere puppet. And this raises the question of just how we structure an order of ministry so that its proper freedom can be coupled to effective modes of accountability.

My second modern poet, Anne Stevenson, also wrote a poem called 'The Minister'. She opens up fascinating and alluring dimensions to the role of presbyter in this description of a conversation between people contemplating a forthcoming funeral:

We're going to need the minister
to help this heavy body into the ground.

But he won't dig the hole;
others who are stronger and weaker will have to do that.
And he won't wipe his nose and his eyes;
others who are weaker and stronger will have to do that.
And he won't bake cakes or take care of the kids –
women's work. Anyway,

what would they do at a time like this
if they didn't do that?

No, we'll get the minister to come
and take care of the words.

He doesn't have to make them up,
he doesn't have to say them well,
he doesn't have to like them
so long as they agree to obey him.
We have to have the minister
so the words will know where to go.
Imagine them circling and circling

the confusing cemetery.
Imagine them roving the earth
without anywhere to rest.[5]

Ordinary people have some kind of a picture of just what it is
that makes a minister. There can be no doubting that. We may
want to dismiss this as fiction or fantasy or illusion but it
definitely exists and can probably be spelled out as follows:

- a minister is the person who stands up to preach, to conduct
  funerals, to baptize children, to conduct weddings, to offer
  bread and wine;
- a minister visits us in our homes and models the Christian life
  for us;
- a minister takes charge of the words and reminds us of a
  dimension to human living which, under the pressures of
  everyday life, is too easily forgotten.

We recognize the person who emerges from this portrait all right.
This is a familiar friend, none other than the proverbial
'archangel Gabriel' whom all circuit stewards long for when they
are looking for a new minister.

This expectation, this understanding of the minister's role, is
easy to parody and dismiss. It is the picture that undergirds the

So often the lay Visitor is a relative or friend to whom You don't confide at all!

oft-repeated and much disapproved-of view that, while a visit from a class leader (or some other church member) is fine, it is the minister's visit that really matters. We, the thinking class of the Methodist Church, have winced at such opinions often enough and used them to justify our intention to broaden and enrich patterns of pastoral care. Just now and again we may even have referred to them in order to justify our view that ministers no longer need visit their flock. After all, if a ministerial visit has the effect of diminishing the value of the pastoral care of lay people for each other, then it does, perhaps, need questioning. In arguing thus, we may unwittingly have gone down a road that, by turning ministers into managers, reconfigures some essential aspects of what we think a presbyter is ordained to do.

I believe that we should look again at our readiness to dismiss these folksy views of the presbyteral role. Essential-practice babies may have been thrown away with our bad-practice bath-water. However crude these views of the ministerial role may be, they do at least reveal a basic expectation on the part of ordinary people that may not be so wide of any benchmark we might want to set.

It is my view that the demystification of the minister's role and the 'democratization' of ministerial activity are among the most serious mistakes that were made in twentieth-century Method-ism. And those of us who purport to have the ministry of the whole people of God, the priesthood of all believers, in mind; or who seek to empower, enable, enfranchise the people of God with our latest theories and theologies; we turn out to be the very people who seem unable or unwilling to listen to the voice of those same people when we so speedily rubbish or dismiss the models of ministry they cherish.

I think the time has come to heed our people and respond to their declared (or suppressed) needs. If we end up rejecting or redefining their understanding of the presbyter then the least we can do is give them some clear reasons why we have decided to do this. As for me, within a few years of the end of my own ministry, I will go on doing it my way. Not out of malice or spite, or in the curmudgeonly spirit of King Canute, but because, until

I have always and still do. Say so student — Visit all Your members:- Your first Year or Ten ask the Rural Council. What Now?

we have done our thinking on this issue, I want our people and our theologians to have a range of models they can look at. I know I am not the only person who thinks as I do and I am glad of that. If we do end up with a different understanding of ministry from the one that attracted me all those years ago then I will accept whatever thinking comes to pass. But at least let us reach that point with our eyes open to what is happening. I really cannot bear the conspiracy of silence or the reactive ways we have done our theology over the years that have allowed a model we could identify readily enough to be eaten away without, as it seems to me, a question being asked.

This is Not So .

As an ex-President of the Conference I have the great privilege to preside at ordination services. I cannot explain the sheer joy that invades my being as I assume this role on behalf of the Connexion. When hands have been duly laid on those who come forward, when prayer has been liberally offered, it falls to me to issue a charge. It is not a complicated matter. It appears on page 308 of *The Methodist Worship Book*, which was published as recently as 1999 and incorporates the best thinking of our Faith and Order Committee over many years prior to that. The charge I hear myself give sums up the thinking of the Church about the nature of the role into which those being ordained have been placed. It is a formula that differs somewhat from the charge issued to me at my ordination but I am more than happy with the assumptions about presbyteral ministry that lie behind it. It could have been written by Geoffrey Chaucer!

> Remember your call.
> Declare the Good News.
> Celebrate the sacraments.
> Serve the needy.
> Minister to the sick.
> Welcome the stranger.
> Seek the lost.
> Be shepherds to the flock of Christ.
> As you exercise mercy, do not forget justice;
> As you minister discipline, do not forget mercy;

that when Christ the Chief Shepherd comes in glory
he may count you among his faithful servants.

My big worry is that the needs of the Church in these times of
shortage have led to developments that put the practice of
ministry at odds with the concepts central to the very ordination
service that launches the ministry of every presbyter in the land.
I hope this volume will address this problem and help the Church
to grapple with a question that goes to the heart of its life and, I
believe, affects its very identity in the wider world beyond it.

I agree with most of this
but some things has been said
that about 'Calvet love's praise'

But I am, like Griffith, quite
unrepentant that the minister is there
as preach, pastor, president at the
sacraments, enabler, counsellor
and representative of the wider
church in the name of Christ.

2

Mind the Gap

JANE LEACH

'When I use a word,' Humpty Dumpty said, in a rather scornful tone, 'it means just what I choose it to mean – neither more nor less.'
'The question is,' said Alice, 'whether you can make words mean so many different things.'
'The question is,' said Humpty Dumpty, 'which is to be the master – that's all.'[1]

One thing about which we are likely to agree is that it is going to be difficult to arrive at a common understanding of what the word 'presbyter' means. Here, then, is my bid, to be master of the word and make it mean what it means for me . . .

Not that this is an attempt to be definitive. Any understanding of presbyteral ministry must be worked out in dialogue with understandings of what it is to be a lay person or a deacon, or a presbyter in another tradition, and those understandings must be at least partly articulated by those who bear those identities. Yet to be a presbyter in the Methodist Church is also to adopt, grow into, interpret, live out, an identity.[2] It is a public identity – a category of person in society that has a collection of assumptions and expectations adhering to it – but as with any public identity, it is also a matter of personal negotiation. To be recognizably a senior tutor in Wesley House, for example, I do not have to be everything that my predecessors were; to be recognizably a presbyter, I am relieved to conclude that I do not have to take on all the expectations of the Christian tradition or the local congregation, but I do need to negotiate with these expectations if I am to be publicly recognized as a presbyter.

The identity of a presbyter must then be worked out in

dialogue both across time in conversation with the Christian tradition and personal biography and, in this place and time, together with all whom I would like to recognize me as a presbyter in the contemporary Church and beyond it.[3]

Only at the top! Unfortunately, it seems that it is not politically correct in the current Methodist climate, at least, to talk about the presbyterate at all. Any attempt to assign a role to our ministers other than that of the ubiquitous *enabler* is held to be an attack upon the priesthood of all believers or upon diaconal ministry or upon the ministry of the whole people of God.

I suggest in this chapter that this sense of threat is based upon one fallacy and one instance of the divorce of our theology from our practice. The fallacy consists in the belief that any suggestion that presbyters have a distinct role to play in the life of the Church and the world is grounded in a view that ministers hold a ministry differing in kind from that of the rest of the people of God.[4] In this chapter, a claim is made for a distinctive and vital role for the presbyterate that does not suggest a ministry differing in kind from that exercised by the rest of the *laos*, but rather, one that self-consciously and publicly and articulately embodies the calling of the baptized.

The instance of the divorce of theology from practice to which I refer is that of the divorce of doing from being. I think that the sense that ministers cannot have any distinctive role without threatening the role of the rest of the *laos* is grounded in a functional definition of what ministers are – people who do certain things. Immediately any task is cordoned off for ministers only, the question is asked, 'Why can't a lay person do that?' In this chapter, I argue that there is nothing a presbyter does that cannot be done by a lay person equally well, if not better at times, yet the presbyter still has a distinctive role to play in the life of the community and is the most appropriate person in normal circumstances to preach, to preside at the Eucharist and to be in pastoral charge of our churches; an argument that I will seek to illuminate using insights from social anthropology about the nature of social identity and the concept of embodiment.

First, though, as a pastoral theologian, I want to begin in a particular context and use a particular method. The method is an action-reflection method that begins with the rich description of a particular context as a social anthropologist would describe it; next it draws upon the insights of a variety of canons of thought before theologically reflecting upon the whole and drawing conclusions about how to be and act.[5]

The place where I want to begin is in a Methodist Circuit, on a Sunday morning, travelling to a preaching appointment with a Circuit Steward to a small rural chapel where I am to play the organ. On that journey we pass one chapel closed five years ago; one chapel thinking of rebuilding though no members of that church actually live in the village; and we arrive at the third chapel – a dilapidated building, an elderly congregation of five.

As we travel home, the Circuit Steward relates to me how she had toyed with abandoning any sermon and instead had thought of engaging the congregation in some kind of reflection on who they are and what, as the Church, they are for; she tells me with exasperation of the lay worker (who had arrived late at the service), and who, after a year, seems to have made no headway at all in helping that church to exercise its ministry as the Church in that place; as we pass the chapel to be rebuilt, she tells me of the minister who is driving the rebuilding scheme and who complains that no one seems able to catch the vision, and this Circuit Steward expresses to me, with real soul-searching, her reservations about the wisdom of rebuilding at all in such circumstances; she tells me of the plans to reshape the Circuit ready for the appointment of a new Superintendent minister next September and of her sense of despair at the current Super's inability to engage with the need to do things differently; and she finishes her somewhat anguished tirade with the question, 'Who is the minister here?'

And how do we interpret such an outburst? Doubtless more information would be helpful to us; more points of view. Maybe the Circuit Steward has axes to grind and scores to settle; maybe she is not well or not seeing things straight. But suppose we take her at her word and ask with her the question, 'Who is the minister here?' and couple that with our question, 'What is a presbyter?'

We could take the view that thank goodness this Circuit Steward is there. And what an endorsement for the ministry of lay people: a lay preacher who is unafraid to abandon form and engage with real issues; a Circuit Steward who is thinking and praying and working towards a new vision of ministry and leadership for her Circuit; a lay person of commitment and perception who can see clearly the way things are and the need for them to be different. And we could rejoice in the ministry of the whole people of God, and suggest that she does Foundation Training and that would be that, except that we would be ignoring the fact that she feels beleaguered and isolated because the Circuit ministers seem unable, in their different ways, to stand in the gap between the now and the not yet, and she who has no training and no authority beyond the Circuit's six-year elected term seems to bear this responsibility alone.

Yet there are two presbyters in that Circuit; they perform the functions of presbyters: they preach, they preside at Communion; they baptize; they chair meetings; they visit the sick; they bury the dead. But this Circuit Steward feels the weight of being the minister here because she perceives that one minister, heading towards retirement, is standing in the now, content enough with things as they are, and the other stands in the not yet, railing against the present for not being the future, and neither seems able to live where this Circuit Steward must live and where we all must live and where all the baptized are called to choose to live – in the present, attentive to the weaving of the new creation.

There are certain tube stations in London where, as the doors open, you will hear the incantation, 'Mind the gap; stand clear of the doors please. Mind the gap.' What I am suggesting in this chapter is that it is the role of the presbyter to mind the gap – the gap between the now and the not yet – self-consciously, publicly and articulately to struggle to discipline ourselves to live in that space in between what we know and what we do not yet know, where God is weaving the future, and to draw others into the kind of attending to the moment that makes room for God to work in the here and now of human lives.

But, I imagine you will say to me, 'Is not that the role of the whole people of God?' Minding the gap, attending to what God is doing in the present; what Paul Tillich called, cultivating the space into which God may speak. Demonstrably a circuit steward can do it; a farmer does it waiting for crops to sprout; a parent does it watching as a life unfolds; a nurse does it, waiting like the crowds before Lazarus' tomb for the words, 'Unbind him and let him go . . .' whether into life or into death . . .

Of course anyone can do it: presbyters hold no ministry differing in kind from that of the rest of the *laos*. What is a presbyter? A presbyter is one whom the Church has recognized as one who is able and willing self-consciously, publicly and articulately to live the life of the baptized so that the baptized can see how they are to be in any particular time and place; so that the baptized have someone to be with them in the gap where they are called to be; not someone with the answers, but someone able and willing visibly to live their life and audibly to articulate their questions and pray aloud the inarticulate prayers of the whole creation as it groans and waits for fulfilment.

In suggesting this to be the role of the presbyter, I am drawing on the concept of embodiment.[6] A key concept in social anthropology is that human beings are not only rational, logical, conscious creatures, but bodies amongst other bodies. Even our experience of the processes of the mind are embodied experiences. We dream, we remember – all in the mind – and yet, as we do, we sweat, we smile, we weep. And, as bodies, we need other bodies. We need to hear and see and taste and touch and smell other bodies being Christian, in order to be Christian ourselves.

So far that tells us that Christians, in order to be Christian, need other Christians. We need to be in touch with those who embody for us, within the creative limits of our space and time, what it is to live the life of the baptized.

The resonance of this when we think about incarnation can hardly be lost on theological minds. The word made flesh *ugh!*

embodies for us what it is, as Pannenberg puts it, to be God when God is human[7] – to be God when God limits Godself to our space and time. And for us to be Godlike – to be recreated in the image of God – we need the word embodied so that we can taste and see and hear and smell and touch within space and time what it is to be fully human. This is what God in Christ is about.

So far, I guess I am on safe ground. But when Paul talks about our being in Christ he is talking about us, too, embodying God, nothing less – because we human beings need Christ and need Christ embodied for us here and now by those who are in Christ. Of course we get it wrong. But sometimes gloriously we get it right and God is made known amongst us.

Presbyters, I am arguing, are first and foremost those we have seen to be in Christ. This is why we say at ordination, 'They are worthy' – worthy through being in Christ. Of course, there are many more people in Christ than those called to be presbyters, but because the Church is a social reality, a group of bodies, in order to function it looks for leaders – those who not only embody its values and way of life, but who can talk about it in the pulpit and in the church council and enact it at the deathbed and through the sacraments.

Anyone can exegete a text, given the training; anyone can perform the technicalities of consecrating bread and wine given a rehearsal. But who is most appropriate to do it? I suggest to you that we need people presiding at the Eucharist who know they stand in the gap between the now and the not yet where grace may be wonderfully at work; I suggest that we need people commending our loved ones to God who know what Sheryl Anderson, Director of the South London Mission, is talking about when she writes, 'I have come to understand that conducting a funeral is not just leading a service; more it is about standing in the place between life and death and guarding the gateway so that the living can look through and not be terrified.'[8] And I suggest that we need people chairing our church councils and preaching in our pulpits who can articulate what they see and hear and taste and smell and touch of God at work amongst their people whom they visit and take trouble to get to know.

ugh! *! ?*

to We do not think in terms of "consecration", do we?

I will give you an embodied example of what I mean: during
the time I was in pastoral charge of a rural chapel in the Fens a
dear woman of 87 called Dora died just before I went to a further
training course, and so I was unable to take her funeral. She was
dear to me because she honoured me as a dwelling place of God
– always telling me to take care of myself and not to do too much
and that she prayed for me. In the last months when she was ill,
I was a regular visitor, and we talked amongst other things about
the depression that was an intermittent feature of her whole life.
And at one point, I said to her, 'Sometimes you just want to curl
up in a ball.' And she stared at me as if the world had changed
colour, and whispered, in wonder, 'You know!'

She recognized me – and I, her. And because she had already
recognized me as someone in whom God dwells, suddenly she
could see that this was true of herself – that she too was a
precious child of God whose place is held between the stars. And
suddenly, I could see it too – knowing her to be so precious,
identifying with her in her illness, suddenly I, too, knew myself
beloved.

I visited her in hospital the next time we met. I had a student
minister with me. It was three o'clock in the afternoon, and no
one had yet washed Dora's face or combed her hair. I drew the
curtains around, found a bowl and soap and a flannel and
washed her face and hands, and combed her hair – not to shame
anyone for not having done it; but because, knowing her to be
the dwelling place of God, I could not leave her unattended.
Having once recognized her the knowledge could not be
unknown and had to be not only acknowledged, but celebrated.
It is one of the most joyful things I have ever been part of –
she smiling at me, and I at her – knowing ourselves, and all
humanity, beloved.

This is what ministry is and it belongs to the whole people of
God – and this story is as much about her ministry to me as it is
about mine to her. But what belongs to the presbyter is to exercise this ministry visibly and to talk about it and enact it in ways
that help others to recognize and participate in and celebrate the
mystery of God as an intimacy in our flesh; ministry does not

belong to presbyters alone any more than to be fully human belongs to Christ alone, but presbyters are publicly promised to it as Christ in Gethsemane, even when the tension between the way things are and the way they are being recreated to be tears us apart . . .

Presbyters are called to live in the gap, not so that others do not have to, but in order that others have someone with whom to do it; so that they have someone embodying the life they need to be living too, so that they have someone who can articulate what is going on; so that they can see and hear and taste and smell and touch how it is they are to live if they are not, as is so easy for all of us to do, to spiral away into idolatry.[9]

And this is not putting ministers on pedestals, asking them to be more perfect than the rest of the *laos*, like rich patrons paying medieval monks to pray so that we do not have to. This is asking those whom we perceive to be living in the gap between the now and the not yet, and who have the gifts and graces, to do it publicly, in the pulpit and the sanctuary and school assembly – visible to the worshipping community and to the wider community, publicly confessing their sins and their need of God and opening their hands to God's future not knowing where it will lead. And we ask them to do it for life, because the life of discipleship is a life-long project on which all of us are embarked; and we give them training to do it in the wisdom of the tradition and in the ways of the world that they may discern the signs of the times and know where the gap is in order to invite others into it; and we authorize them to do it and promise to uphold them in it because it is a damn difficult thing to do and if we did not dedicate some people to concentrate upon it, we should lose our way and be unable to be a royal priesthood on behalf of the world which is the calling of the whole people of God.

And if the ministry of the whole people of God is a priestly ministry – interceding on behalf of the world; putting ourselves within the stream of grace that we may be channels of grace to others – then presbyteral ministry is a priestly ministry. It is an embodiment of, a focus for our attention that reminds us that we are a people who live in the gap between the now and the not yet;

in the place where God is active, so that we may be channels of grace for the life of the world.

And we are a royal priesthood, a chosen people, not to privilege us above other peoples, but to draw others into the gap between the now and the not yet, free from the tyranny of past and future, where the timeless may intersect with time and God may be known. And likewise those of us called to the presbyterate are chosen, not to privilege us above other peoples, but to draw others into this place and into this quality of attention that makes room for the Spirit of God, not to draw attention to ourselves, but to Christ in whom earth and heaven are one.

Maybe this seems too high a calling. Maybe to embody God, as Christ does, seems too high a calling, for, as Douglas Davies argues in his *Studies in Pastoral Theology and Social Anthropology*, although Christians are keen to dwell on the mystery of the incarnation they are oddly ill at ease in comparing the life of Jesus with their own life, becoming distracted by the sense of a moral gulf between the life of Christ and their own life.[10]

Putting morality aside for one moment, when we allow Christ to dwell in us, then we find that we recognize him embodied in others and most wonderfully in ourselves, no longer regarding anyone from a human point of view,[11] but seeing them and ourselves, both now of infinite value, and not yet fully open to all the fullness of God.

> To communicate with Mars, converse with spirits,
> To report the behaviour of the sea monster,
> Describe the horoscope, haruspicate or scry,
> Observe disease in signatures, evoke
> Biography from the wrinkles of the palm
> And tragedy from fingers; release omens
> By sortilege, or tea leaves, riddle the inevitable
> With playing cards, fiddle with pentagrams
> Or barbituric acids, or dissect
> The recurrent image into pre-conscious terrors –
> To explore the womb, or tomb, or dreams; all these are usual

Pastimes and drugs, and features of the press:
And always will be, some of them especially
When there is distress of nations and perplexity
Whether on the shores of Asia, or in the Edgware Road.
Men's curiosity searches past and future
And clings to that dimension. But to apprehend
The point of intersection of the timeless
With time, is an occupation for the saint –
No occupation either, but something given
And taken, in a lifetime's death in love,
Ardour and selflessness and self-surrender.
For most of us, there is only the unattended
Moment, the moment in and out of time,
The distraction fit, lost in a shaft of sunlight,
The wild thyme unseen, or the winter lightning
Or the waterfall, or music heard so deeply
That it is not heard at all, but you are the music
While the music lasts. These are only hints and guesses,
Hints followed by guesses; and the rest
Is prayer, observance, discipline, thought and action.
The hint half guessed, the gift half understood, is Incarnation.[12]

(*Ts Eliot*)

?

In our generation, I fear, we make light of presbyteral ministry, not least through the lack of funding for appropriate training and a lack of discernment about those whom we would really ask to do this thing for us; and in doing so we make light of the ministry of the whole people of God because those called to presbyteral ministry are called to embody and articulate the life of the baptized. We are called to be saints – not to be saintly, or pious, but to be saints in the sense that Paul means when he addresses his congregations who are fighting each other and relapsing into all kinds of sin and seeking their security in the past or the future. He writes to *hoi hagioi* – the saints who are in Corinth, Colossae, Thessalonike, Cambridge, Cromer, Downham Market – and invites them, as *he* does, most publicly and self-consciously and articulately, to live in the gap between the now and the not yet, where, free from past and future, time interacts with timelessness and the fullness of God is pleased to dwell.

'What is a presbyter?' I contend that a presbyter is one who is promised to mind the gap between the now and the not yet, that we and all the baptized and the whole creation may, in the words of the letter to the saints in Ephesus,

> be strong to grasp what is the breadth and length and height and depth of Christ's love, and to know it, though it is beyond knowledge. So may you be filled with the very fullness of God.[13]

3

Where is the Minister?
The Place of Ministry

Philip Luscombe

Ministers – lay or ordained – must minister in a particular place. This does not have to be a geographical location: sector ministers may focus on a place of work or leisure. All ministry, however, is specific. Both lay and ordained minister to, with, for, or alongside a particular place or group of people. In most denominations the ordained minister is licensed to a parish, or chosen by a congregation. Although the parish model of the Church is very different from the gathered or associational model, both share an understanding of the relation of the minister to locality.[1] The minister works in one particular place, and even when this is modified, usually by economic necessity, to include a group of churches or parishes, the theory of the relationship remains the same. This is significantly different from Methodism's model of the minister as the 'connexional person' working in the local setting. In this chapter I will explore the Methodist Church's understanding of connexion, and the way this has been worked out in the familiar circuit system of British Methodism. How much is our picture of ordained ministry shaped by our understanding of the Church? And is the model a help or hindrance to the mission of the Church?

The Connexional Principle

The relationship between minister and congregation in Methodism is a complex one, both in practice and theology. The

Methodist understanding is not adequately described by either
the congregational principle that the whole Church subsists in
the local and that therefore the local congregation has God's
authority to call and ordain, or the Catholic position that 'the
local church' is the whole diocese, so that the Church is defined
by all those in communion with the local bishop through his
college of priests. *ₖ Pope ?*

'The connexional principle' is defined in 'Called to Love and
Praise', the 1999 statement of the British Methodist Church on
the nature of the Christian Church. According to that report it
involves the mutuality and interdependence of all parts of the
whole Church, together with the attempt to give the greatest
possible degree of autonomy to each part of the Church. So
subsidiarity at local, circuit and district level is commended. In
John Wesley's day, the connexion stood for those groups that
had voluntarily connected themselves to Wesley and his work,
but as Methodism developed from a religious society into a
church, so the concept of connexion needed to develop in order
to hold together the sometimes competing understandings of the
central authority and the local churches. Today the Church
aspires to a balance between central planning and 'policing' and
local freedom and flexibility:

> [Local autonomy] is necessary if they [churches, circuits,
> districts] are to express their own cultural identity and to
> respond to local calls of mission and service in an appropriate
> way. But their dependence on the larger whole is also neces-
> sary for their own continuing vitality and well being. Such
> local autonomy may also need to be limited from time to time
> in the light of the needs of the whole Church.[2]

Note that subsidiarity within the connexion is carefully defined.
Methodism is not an association of individual churches which
have chosen to pool their sovereignty.

For most Methodists an obvious outworking of connexionalism is found in its deployment of the ordained ministry. All
Methodist ministers are stationed. The retired are still officially

listed as attached to a particular circuit; those in Local Appointment have their stationing reviewed regularly, and although they are often not free to move geographically, the place and shape of their ministry is still a matter for the Methodist Conference. Similarly those in sector appointments are also stationed by Conference, although as Clifford Bellamy describes in his chapter, the Church has often been slow to appreciate or exploit their particular ministry. Most clearly the itinerant circuit minister holds within him or herself the tension of representing the whole Church whilst ministering in particular localities.

Between Pulpit and Pew: Local Methodism

The following two quotations speak of the Methodism of 30 years ago. Both concern areas where Methodism was *a* if not *the* dominant religious force, and both were written by not unsympathetic outsiders. The first is an optimistic remembrance from Gareth Jones, an Anglican theologian:

> Back in the Black Country in the 1960's and early 70's, I was far more conscious of the Methodist Church than I was of the Church of England. Not only did there seem to be a large number of Methodist churches, but they also seemed to possess a vitality and a tradition that was welcoming and embracing. In short, there was a genuine fit between the Methodist spirit and the character of life in the Midlands.[3]

Jones puts into words what we would like to see as the myth of our past, the Methodist spirit genuinely enabling the true spirit of the local identity to be articulated. From a different part of the country, however, David Clark, an anthropologist, probes a little more deeply.

> The more closely we examine the transformations which have occurred within official Methodism, or the sacred culture, as we have preferred to call it, the more apparent it becomes that the people of Staithes have devoted considerable energy

to the task of elaborating a religious system congruent
with other, more broadly based communal norms and values.
On many occasions this has brought them into conflict
with the guardians of Methodism . . . Ministers were, and are,
frequently perceived as interfering 'foreigners', who, un-
acquainted with local conditions and attitudes, attempt to
assert their will over that of the village populace. As one
woman said of the minister in 1975: 'There's a lot in the village
don't like him. When he came he wanted us to build a
new chapel at the Lane End and for all three [chapels] to get
together. That's when the trouble started. Before that we all
used to get on fine.' [They didn't of course, but that is a long
story . . .]⁴

(Staithes has a little unnuwal in several ways.)

Clark's book, *Between Pulpit and Pew*, remains both funny and
deeply depressing as he describes his year-long stay in a
Yorkshire fishing village, with the local people defending their
'traditional' understanding of Methodism (the Sunday School
Anniversary, the Fishermen's Choir and the several chapels)
against all comers: the poor Probationer minister sent to live in
the village; the Superintendent, remote in the small town a few
miles away; the Darlington District, and occasionally even
the connexion in London. For Staithes, connexionalism has
become the minister as 'interfering foreigner'. This fault line in
practice runs deep within Methodism, perhaps back through the
nineteenth century and its controversies over the Wesleyan
Pastoral Office and the need for a body of pastors independent of
particular congregations who ruled the church. Perhaps back to
Wesley himself and his assistants or helpers moving rapidly
between the circuits.

I asked a friend for his recollection of Methodism in the north-
east in the 1920s:

The Minister seemed very remote. Of course in the village,
without adequate transport, he was geographically five
miles distant. In addition, he lived in a large detached house
with a live-in maid. He received his full title at all times . . . He

stipend £250 a year.

visited the village once a fortnight [on Thursday evening], apart from the one Sunday a quarter when he came to administer communion. *But if you knew your stuff you could visit every member. (David Fo— 1956-62.*

The Connexion and the Circuits

We need to separate out two different levels of assumptions about the connexion and connexionalism.

There are independent Methodists, but it is difficult for us to divorce our understanding of what it means to be a Methodist from connexionalism. In his spirited defence of the connexion,[5] Brian Beck lists a number of the interactions between connexionalism and the Methodist understanding of ministry. Connexionalism and itinerancy have been intimately linked since the very earliest beginnings of Methodism. Wesley's original concept was of *monthly* itinerancy and he commented that, 'I wish we had no circuit with fewer than three preachers in it or less than four hundred miles' riding in four weeks.'[6] In the eighteenth century itinerancy was intended to prevent preachers becoming absorbed in pastoral care to the detriment of the nation-wide mission. Can there be a modern equivalent of these ideas? Brian Beck suggests that it might be found in the freedom of Methodist ministers to be able to function where there is no congregation as yet or in areas beyond the local congregation – beyond their geographical, financial or imaginative reach. Connexionalism, he claims, can enable the mission of the Church allowing the Church to minister to new geographical areas or new 'sectors' of society. *They were not ministers! or pastors*

In Wesley's day frequent changes of ministerial appointment were understood to guard both pastor and congregation against collusion in heresy or decline. Frequent change, in itself, however, provides no guarantee against collusion – the former Secretary of Conference points out, perhaps wistfully, that a strong central authority is also required; and we may well doubt if such a structure is possible or even desirable today.

The practical detachment from the local required by itinerancy, together with the (comparatively) strong sense of

? No who pays ?

No! To prevent collusion! – Wesley said so!!

They were societies Not congregations at this stage.

also a sense of an order.

central belonging which connexionalism provides, have always in the past combined to give a strong sense of the 'brotherhood' of the ministry. There were of course negative effects – gatherings of ministers can still sometimes feel like clubs for the boys – but positively the concept of belonging has at its best given ordained ministers a larger identity and an awareness of themselves as more than independent freelance operators. Many have wished to see this identity as similar to belonging to a religious order.

So far our comments on connexionalism could be understood and shared by the vast majority of Methodists across the world. For British Methodists, however, the connexional principle is made real in the local area by the circuit. The authority of the Superintendent and the circuit compared to the local church and the stationing of ministers to a circuit rather than to individual churches would, for many, represent the defining characteristics of Methodism. Clearly the circuit is not essential; circuits are comparatively rare within the United Methodist Church, which nonetheless remains committed to the value of connexionalism. In Britain, although the polity of circuit organization may remain remote to many people in Methodist congregations, most do understand that they share 'their' minister with other churches, that local preachers conduct many of their services, and that they are forced to pay the circuit assessment each quarter. In Britain at least it is through the circuit that connexional polity is expressed locally.

There are many recent reports on ministry, stationing and the organization of the Church. Few do more than note that connexionalism means that ministers are stationed to circuits rather than to individual pastorates. I am not aware of any serious recent discussion of the theological justification of circuit ministry as opposed to the more general principle of connexionalism.

The End of Circuit Ministry

A passing comment in 'The Ministry of the People of God' reminds contemporary readers of an older model of circuit ministry.

> Traditionally the Methodist minister in rural and many urban areas was available to any particular church in his circuit or section only for limited periods on specific days. Frequently he acted almost as a chaplain, who visited some of the churches from time to time and worked intensively in the period available in areas of ministry considered to be of the greatest importance, leaving the effective oversight of the churches between his visits to local leaders. During the twentieth century, the rapid improvement in communications and ease of travel have dramatically affected the relationships between ministers and congregations in all social settings. Sometimes this has led to undue dependence upon and unrealistic expectations of ministers, and to excessive stress in the life-style of ordained persons.[7]

There may be a danger here of looking back towards a golden age which never really existed, but the picture as painted does hold together a number of key Methodist emphases. The preacher or minister has a unique relationship to the society or congregation. The difference is not primarily a function of the number of churches for which the individual minister takes responsibility. Instead there is, as we implied earlier, a theology of minister as missionary holding together Wesley's distinctive concern both to reach out to new areas, but also to feed and sustain those brought into the new societies. Minister and congregation work effectively together because they have their own differentiated tasks. The minister, not least because more often absent than present, both enables and requires the ministry of the whole people of God. Equally during times when the minister is present the emphasis is to work with and equip the congregation for their own ministry. Becoming deeply involved in pastoral care is seen as a distraction to be avoided wherever possible. To use today's language, ordained ministry has the task of mission not maintenance. *[handwritten: Ans what Does that mean? give examples!]*

But as the quotation suggests, this vision of circuit ministry has been killed by the telephone and the car. Today, improved communications allow the ordained minister to be called in as the expert, allowing or forcing the minister into the role of professional pastoral carer, which is very far from Wesley's original conception of his helpers. This might be simply the inevitable working out of the change from new movement into settled denomination. The danger is that what remains of the circuit system is a second-rate version of conventional pastoral ministry, made inevitably ineffective by the number of churches which each minister must serve, no longer as a Methodist preacher in full partnership with the whole people, but as the overworked copy of a denominational pastor or priest. Such a change has diminished the ministry of both lay and ordained.

Before moving on, it is worth noting the irony in the fact that the evocative description in 'The Ministry of the People of God' of what has been lost from circuit ministry – lost from the ministry of both the ordained and the lay ministers – occurs as a justification for the role of Ministers in Local Appointment. The report was seeking a favourable reception for what was then a new concept within Methodism, the idea that ordained ministers need not be itinerant. But, claims 'The Ministry of the People of God', MLAs are only like the circuit ministers of old in not being available to each congregation at all times; and anyway, the paragraph concludes, brutally disregarding its own comments about unrealistic expectations and stress, today's ordinary circuit minister *is* always available and so can cover for the MLA, who will only ever form a minority within the staff of the circuit.

[handwritten: the argument is not clear here.]

Flexible Patterns in the Circuits

If the Church properly understood the theology of a connexional ministry, then that of itself would provide for, even require, the flexibility in the use and deployment of ministers the demand for which has been a feature of Methodist reports since the 1960s. Sector ministry and Ministry in Other Appointments (a particularly revealing usage, of course, 'other' than normative, 'other' than serving the paramount needs of the settled congregations) would be seen as the natural outworking of Wesley's travellers two centuries later. However, the twentieth and twenty-first centuries view the Methodist Church through a lens provided by the nineteenth century rather than the eighteenth. Hence the need for reports such as 'The Ministry of the People of God' and 'The Ministry of the People of God in the World' – again, a wonderfully telling title: where else could God's people live, let alone minister? Yet another report, 'Flexible Patterns of Ministry', did its best to return the Church to a concept of ministers who minister rather than maintain, but even so it could not avoid falling into many of the traps awaiting the unwary. There is a rather sad note appended to the published version of the report:

> In receiving the Report Conference recognized that the exercise of presbyteral ministry does not take place wholly within the church. By their ordination, [and, we might add, by their common baptism] ministers have an obligation to share in God's mission in the world.[8]

Unfortunately the report fails to differentiate properly between an itinerant ministry at the service of the Church as institution, and an itinerant ministry serving God's mission. I do not want to be misunderstood here. I am not claiming that the Church is merely a human institution and that therefore its needs have little priority, nor – even more emphatically – do I wish to claim that the individual minister (or the college of presbyters), rather than the Church, can be guaranteed to discern the will of God. Instead I am attempting here carefully to differentiate between the voracious needs of the Church and its circuits and the original purpose for which itinerancy was instituted. The availability of ministers for stationing so that the pastoral needs of

[handwritten annotation: Rea Lenton on what reference Hem.]

stable congregations may be met is a legitimate aspiration of the Church. It is, however, a far cry from the itinerancy of preachers travelling to spread scriptural holiness throughout the land. A missionary theology of ministry so easily becomes in practice chaplaincy to the cosy church club, and of itself the circuit system has not prevented such changes. *[handwritten: WHY always denigrate the Church?]*

This discussion suggests a number of questions:

- As the Methodist Church has changed from a connexion of fluid and ever-changing societies into a denomination, has its understanding of ordained ministry developed in parallel? The original differentiated partnership in ministry between the members of the society and the itinerant helper is widely praised by Methodism's ecumenical partners. It is a pattern which is difficult to sustain in a new age. Can the circuit system of deep partnership in ministry be rescued from its near destruction by the telephone and the car?

- *[handwritten: Just it assumed the CfE]* Itinerancy was originally intended to serve God's mission as understood by John Wesley. As the Methodist movement grew and developed an itinerant ministry helped the emerging Methodist churches to remain flexible and responsive, and helped to sustain a coherent Methodist identity. More recently itinerancy has well served the needs of a settled church, which still seeks to give a priority to mission. Given the changes in society, family life and career expectations (for both ministers and their spouses), can itinerancy be reinvented once more to serve a new century? *[handwritten: It is as Dead as a Duck!]*

- Methodism has benefited greatly from ecumenical conversations and insights, not least in the way in which it has borrowed and incorporated into its own understanding much ecumenical theology of ministry and ordination. At present the older concept of the itinerant Methodist preacher and the ecumenical understanding of the representative presbyter sit together within Methodism, perhaps uneasily. How might the different insights be brought creatively together?

In the late 1990s the report 'Flexible Patterns of Ministry' sought to open the subject for debate within Methodism. It can be criticized for its concentration on ministry in the service of the Church, rather than the world. On the other hand 'Flexible Patterns' has begun to understand that if the mission of the Church is to be advanced then not only must the concept of the normative ministerial appointment be discarded, but – given the place where the Church finds itself today – any experimentation must involve a partnership between the ordained and the whole of the Church of which they are part. Circuits are not necessarily an incubus to mission, but can return to something of the original vision for them. Malcolm Braddy's words are rightly much quoted:

> Through their ordination and reception into Full Connexion, ministers are to be the focus of the church's apostolic mission to the world. To achieve this, they will have to be released from a maintenance ministry in the church. Time after time ministers are frustrated because they are placed in churches which have no spark and take no risks. Full connexion provides for the circuits the reassurance that they are not alone and that any experimentation in maintenance, mission, evangelism and social caring has the support of other Methodists.[9]

The Place of Ministry

The ambivalence about place which we have described is probably a necessary and unavoidable component of Methodism. John Vincent can write that incarnation means 'digging in', and 'Called to Love and Praise' can demand 'the greatest possible degree of autonomy' for all levels of the Church, but in practice part of the character of Methodism is the tension between the local and the central. This is, after all, only the way we work out the necessary incarnational meeting between the universal truths of the gospel and the particular needs or insights of the local place. It is probably also inevitable that for us this tension will be embodied most sharply within the ordained minister. Elsewhere

in this book Jane Leach writes of the gap which ministers are
called to mind. One of the bridges which the ordained are called
to build is between the general and the particular; between a
local vision and that of the Church universal. This is hardly
unique to Methodism, but the way in which Methodism has
embodied this tension is self-consciously distinctive. The connexional principle helps to make the issue unavoidable and
potentially creative. The British working out of the connexional
principle through circuits and circuit ministers is one response to
the more universal issue.

The ordained minister is the connexional person in the local
place and very often, although not invariably, also the one who
must mediate local understandings to the highest courts of the
Church. Ministers are called to carry within themselves the
polarities of connexion and locality. Whilst earlier understandings – certainly so far as the Wesleyans were concerned –
probably tilted the balance decisively in the direction of connexional authority, contemporary theology demands a more equal
balance. Brian Beck has pointed out the danger of the old
Wesleyan theory of the Pastoral Office. By developing a strong
and independent theology of ordained ministry alongside a
Methodist understanding of the church, church and ministry
were condemned to unending conflict. As we have seen, such
tensions could not be removed simply by the careful compromise
of the Deed of Union. We still struggle to understand how the
concept of 'no priesthood differing in kind' can be held together
with a connexional understanding of ministry for and on behalf
of the whole Church. The endless series of Conference debates
on the relation of the priesthood of all believers to the celebration
of the Eucharist only serves to demonstrate the point. Brian Beck
poses the dilemma in these terms: 'we still have not settled in our
collective mind how to relate pastoral responsibility for the life
of the church to the structures of representative government nor
how to affirm that the responsibility given in ordination is shared
with lay people without being taken away from ministers'.[10]

Ministers and ministry cannot exist in a vacuum. The question
'what is a minister?' always relates to the context and location of

ministry. The way in which Methodism has developed from a connexion of religious societies into a denomination of the Church raises specific issues for those called to exercise ministry as Methodists. There are great and unresolved contradictions within Methodist understanding and practice.

Connexional and Local

Methodism can choose to engage thoroughly and realistically with the locality. This would not necessarily involve any great change to the connexional principle. It would imply the fleshing out of current aspirations towards local autonomy. It would also involve a careful look at the theology of the circuit. Are circuits about promoting the mission of the Church within a broad area, or are they primarily concerned to minister to settled congregations? At their worst do circuits simply prop up the declining remnants of nineteenth-century Methodism's attempt to create a parish system to rival that of the Church of England? In an ecumenical age does Methodism waste its energy in promoting circuit links between Methodists, who living in different localities often share little in the way of common mission? Might this energy instead be freed for a wholehearted ecumenical engagement with the spirit of the locality?

One of the defining features of British Methodism is the stationing of ministers to circuits rather than to individual churches, or even to groups of churches. The intention is clearly to emphasize connexionality and sharing among and between churches, to remove the ordained staff from an over-close involvement with the local church, and to promote missionary and other initiatives beyond the local church.

Underlying this issue is an even more fundamental one which concerns the primary role of the ordained. Wesley used his helpers to go where they were most needed, for him that was both to help equip and build the Methodist societies and in mission to those outside. These were the most urgent needs; there was no time for pastoral care; that would be attended to by others. In a settled church priorities change. The pastoral role of

the minister is taken for granted, but there is often debate about
the other roles. Should the ordained minister help equip lay
Christians for their missionary role, the minister working
primarily within the church community, or is it the role of the
ordained to work outside the fixed structures, with the support
of their congregations? The circuit system probably lends itself
more easily to the former role than the latter. So that one answer
to my question of 'where is the minister?' is inside the church
helping others to work in the locality.

The Missionary Circuit

A few years ago the Anglican Church in Wakefield reinvented
itself as the *Missionary* Diocese of Wakefield. This represented a
real attempt to rethink how the structures of the Church ought to
be organized in order to serve contemporary Britain. Could
Methodist circuits attempt to recreate for today the vision of
Wesley and the first few generations? It would be a daunting
exercise. A truly connexional church, with a genuinely itinerant
ministry, would look very different from the Methodist Church
as we know it. The grain of truth behind the attempt to understand Methodist ministers as belonging to a religious order is
that Wesley's travelling preachers were certainly not (to borrow
Catholic terminology) 'secular' clergy. Their primary place of
service was neither a local congregation nor a group of congregations. The immediate missionary needs of the Church
demanded something different. All new religious movements
have to face the challenge of the second and future generations.
British Methodism has been slow to write its theology of the
settled church.[11] Practically the transformation from society to
church was complete many decades ago; the last remnants of the
old language have now all but disappeared. Our theology of
ministry lags behind.

An alternative answer to my question might then be suggested
by the traditional Methodist terminology. The *itinerant* or
travelling preacher might be just that: ordained and set apart
from the concerns of the local congregations to meet wider

[handwritten top-left: This is Very confusing? and I fear quite Unrealistic ...]

[handwritten top-right: Many of our local preachers are 47¾%]

needs, either within or outside the structures of the Church. By contrast the *local* preacher as a lay minister would help each local congregation to respond to local needs and challenges.

[handwritten right margin: relative busy people]

I suggest that we must either take the first option above and integrate ourselves and our ministers fully into one or other of the normal denominational patterns, or, much more radically, search for a genuine circuit ministry and form of itinerancy for this century. Not – as all the reports assume – in order to better serve the needs of the Church, but rather to serve God's mission.

It is often remarked that the model of a minister with pastoral charge of a number of churches is chronically ineffective, at the best, a recipe for managing decline.[12] This seems to me undeniably the case so long as we regard Methodist ministers as primarily ministering to settled congregations of which they have pastoral charge. If, however, the old Methodist partnership in ministry can be recreated, where lay and ordained share in both the mission of the Church and the care and maintenance of its congregations, then we can once again begin to engage in a positive sense with the tension between the local spirit and the catholic truth of the gospel.

[handwritten: The 'Preachers' were Not ordained Normally.]

[handwritten: Frankly this is poor stuff & why oh why wasn't a historian asked to Vet it? AW]

[handwritten: When will we stop looking to the eighteenth century? We don't live there now.]

[handwritten lower-left: Phil was at Queen's — a brilliant Scientist. His book on Science & Religion was Very good indeed.]

[handwritten: What — does one pay it off Money? Who pays all these marvellous itinerant people?]

4

Calling or Cop-out?
Sector Ministry Today

CLIFFORD BELLAMY

'Few innovations in the life of the Church in recent years can have caused as much controversy – even, perhaps, resentment – as the introduction in the late Sixties of the SECTOR MINISTRY.'[1] That statement was written over a quarter of a century ago. The purpose of this chapter is to consider whether sector ministry remains a matter of controversy and resentment today or whether it is now accepted as a valid form of ordained ministry.

History

Although sector ministry was not introduced until 1968, for many years before that there had been a number of ministers each year who were granted 'permission to serve' external organizations such as universities, schools and church-based or church-affiliated organizations like the British and Foreign Bible Society and Toc H. In 1932, at the time of Methodist Union, there were 18 ministers who had 'permission to serve'. Over the following years the number of applications for 'permission to serve' steadily increased. This created a problem.

> With new opportunities in education and other ecumenical agencies the list of applications to serve continued to grow annually. The number of cases seemed to be threatening our normal pattern. The Church was worried. While some

ministers . . . were given permission, others were refused and in consequence some resigned.[2] *afmit it.*

Many were just fed up !! let us admit it.

For many, resignation was not an easy option. To be driven to resignation because of a desire to exercise one's ministry in a non-conventional setting (i.e. outside the 'normative' circuit system) could be both bewildering and traumatic. The problem was not just a dilemma for individual ministers but also for the Church. What was the status of those ministers who had resigned because they had been refused, or believed they would be refused, 'permission to serve'? Was it really in the Church's interests to see ministers resign because they felt called to exercise a ministry outside the circuit system? Something needed to be done. That 'something' was the introduction of sector ministry.

If this gives the impression that sector ministry was introduced for negative or defensive reasons, that was only partly true. Of equal, if not greater, importance was that the Methodist Church itself began to realize that 'the church is becoming increasingly remote from wide areas of life as it is lived in the sectors'.[3] There was a real sense of mission in the introduction of sector ministry.

Before charting its history it is appropriate to explain what the Church means by a 'sector'. The original explanation, given in the report of the Commission on the Church's Ministries in the Modern World in 1968, was that

> In the development of modern society there is a new and increasing complexity. Most people are now called upon to live in a number of different 'worlds' which are largely independent of each other. They play a different role in each world. They work with a different group in each of these areas. In addition to home and family these include work and industry, social services, education etc. and it is to these distinct areas which we refer in the use of the word 'sector'. When we talk about the church in a sector we mean the company of Christians there, the community which Christians discover and create within their sector.[4]

The 1968 Conference agreed to the appointment of a Committee for Ministry in the Sectors. This began work a year later, with a full-time secretary. The committee was charged 'to explore opportunities for ministry in sectors of life other than neighbourhood congregations'. Applications to serve in a sector appointment were channelled, in the first instance, through this committee.

In 1977 a report to the Conference from the Joint Working Party appointed by the Division of Ministries and the Faith and Order Committee expressed the view (which the Conference accepted) that 'those who are now called "sector ministers" should be included in a wider class to be described as "ministers in other appointments", i.e. in appointments not wholly within the control of the Methodist Church'.[5] Though it was now nine years since sector ministry had been introduced, it is interesting to note the report's acknowledgement that 'It is certainly believed by some that the existence of "sector ministry" disrupts the unity of the Methodist ministry by creating a class of ministers who are not wholly subject to the discipline of Conference' and that 'suspicion of "sector ministers" still lingers in some places'.[6]

In 1988, the Commission on the Ministry of the People of God acknowledged the 'persistent opinion within some parts of the Methodist Church that [sector ministers] are doing a job which could equally well be done by lay people'.[7] However, the Commission also made the point that

> Conference has examined this viewpoint on a number of occasions and each time has reaffirmed its commitment to ministry in the Sectors. Some of the work done by those working in this area is innovative and pioneering; some arises from a deep sense of call and commitment to a particular sector; some is an indication of specific skills which some of our ministers possess or have been encouraged to acquire. Much of it brings new insights and resources into the life of the churches.[8]

The Commission recommended a return to the designation

'sector ministry' in place of 'ministers in other appointments'.[9] That recommendation was accepted by the Conference. There has been no further specific consideration of sector ministry since 1988.

Section 74 of the Standing Orders of the Methodist Church sets out the current rules concerning sector ministry. SO 740(1) provides that ministry in sector appointments 'includes full-time ministries in such areas of community life as education, industry and the social services whether exercised in organisations subsidiary or ancillary to the Methodist Church or otherwise'. The criteria for appointment, set out in SO 743(1), provide that

> In considering an initial application from a minister for a ministry in such an appointment the committee shall give particular attention to: (i) the rightness of the appointment for a full and proper exercise of the calling of an ordained minister, such as the exercise of a pioneering or experimental ministry; (ii) the minister's personal qualifications for the appointment; (iii) his or her continued willingness to observe the discipline of the Methodist Church.[10]

One of the main reasons why sector ministry has been under the microscope so often over the years has been because of the failure of the wider church to accept its validity. We turn next to consider some of the reasons for this.

Theology

'The attempt to find a theology of the sector ministry has been hamstrung because many different kinds of appointment have been lumped together in one ragbag.'[11] The first point to be made is fundamental. There is a *single* Order of Presbyters. That this is so is unarguable. At the ordination service the President says to the ordinand: 'God has called you into *the* Order of Presbyters among his people.'[12] A 1975 report declared that 'ministers are ordained not for the *circuit* ministry but for the *Ministry*. Thus the church puts its seal on the minister's claim that he is called by

God. We acknowledge that this call is dynamic, capable of a variety of expression.'[13] In 1988 the point was made again that 'There is one ordained ministry. Those who are based in the circuits, together with all other Methodist ministers, participate in it equally, and together constitute its unity.'[14] The question, therefore, is not 'is there a theology of sector ministry?' but 'is sector ministry compatible with Methodism's theology of ordained ministry?'

So far as Methodism's theology of ordained ministry is concerned, three aspects are clear. First, that the call of God is central. The Deed of Union proclaims that 'It is the universal conviction of the Methodist people that the office of the Christian ministry depends upon the call of God.' All subsequent reports and statements received or adopted by the Conference have reaffirmed this to be the case.

Second, that the ordained minister is 'Christ's ambassador and the representative of the whole people of God'.[15] 'In their office the calling of the whole Church is focused and represented, and it is their responsibility as *representative* persons to lead the people to share with them in that calling. In this sense they are the sign of the presence and ministry of Christ in the Church and through the Church to the world.'[16] It has been said that 'Ordination gives a recognizable office to a person which others in the church [and, it must equally be said, outside the church] are prepared to acknowledge.'[17] The ordination service makes it clear that 'office' and 'authority' are conferred upon a presbyter at ordination. Ordination is thus a leadership issue.

Third, that the ordained person is an 'enabler'. This role is crucial. Mackie argues that 'if all Christians are faithfully and effectively to fulfil their ministry, then it is necessary for some to be set apart for the specific purpose of seeing that the whole church does its job. It is this "enabling" function which is part of the meaning of ordination'.[18] This enabling work can be carried out not only by teaching and encouragement given within the Church but also outside the Church by standing alongside Christians as they seek to live out their faith in the world. In 1970 the Commission on the Church's Ministries in the Modern

World expressed the view that 'An ordained minister in a sector may be more conscious of his role as an "enabler", a co-ordinator and a resource person, especially in biblical, theological and ethical questions.'[19]

Given these essential components of Methodism's theology of ordination, is sector ministry compatible with them? Chapman argues that it is not:

> That Christians should exercise a ministry at their place of work and reflect theologically about their employment seems obvious. But what more can presbyters offer in the sectors when the charismata they have received at ordination are appropriate to their presbyteral responsibility towards the ecclesial community.[20]

This view is flawed in two respects. Firstly, Chapman's use of the expression 'presbyteral responsibility' suggests a wholly functional understanding of ordained ministry. Methodism does not hold to a narrow functional understanding of ordained ministry. Ordination defines what a person *is* as well as what a person *does*. In 1977 the Report of the Joint Working Party appointed by the Division of Ministries and the Faith and Order Committee expressed the view that

> the theological issue has become plain. On the view of the ordained ministry as simply a collection of functions exercised by individuals within the Church . . . there is no case for the continuance of the 'sector ministry', since the functions of an ordained minister can be fulfilled in the 'sector' by lay people . . . On the view of the ordained ministry as focusing, bringing together and representing the ministries of the whole people of God, the case for the 'sector ministry' is made out, since it is the ordained ministry which brings together, represents and focuses the ministries of the Church in the sense required.[21]

Secondly, Chapman's use of the word 'towards' suggests that the ordained minister's responsibilities and functions are to be exercised exclusively 'within' the ecclesial community. We have already noted that Methodism understands the ordained minister to be a 'representative' and an 'ambassador'. Whilst there may be representative and ambassadorial responsibilities 'within' the church, the ordained minister's 'representative' and 'ambassadorial' responsibilities 'on behalf of' the church are of equal if not greater importance. The ordained minister is a representative in the church *and* in the world.

> The Conference . . . has declared the 'representative' view to be an essential part of the truth. By doing so it has implied the further judgment that the concept of 'sector ministry' is theologically valid, and in accordance with the teaching of the Methodist Church.[22]

We noted earlier that Methodism understands the ordained minister to be an 'enabler'. Some have argued that, far from 'enabling', sector ministry usurps the ministry of lay people whose particular call is to ministry in the world. It has been said that the presence of sector ministry contains the implied judgement that the laity are not in fact being and/or are not capable of being effective ministers in the secular world.

The understanding behind sector ministry is that it should be an aid to the ministry of lay people in their secular spheres, not a means of undermining it. In 1968, the Commission on the Church's Ministries in the World acknowledged that 'The Ministry of laymen will be the principal means of Christian impact in the sectors' but also identified that

> The problem is that the Christians in the sector are often unrelated to each other, and their gifts and experience uncoordinated. They often lack the opportunity to consult with those who can help them to develop Christian insights within the context of their sector.[23]

Fennell argues that

> the minister working in a particular sector is a gathering point

for Christians working with him . . . he can help to co-ordinate their efforts so that together they can better be the people of God where they are. Thus the ministry of laymen is not devalued but made more effective because of the servant-leadership of the minister.[24]   *but do they actually do it ?*

As Clark has more recently pointed out, 'the evidence suggests that the presence of an ordained person seems to liberate not repress lay people working through their vocation'.[25]

The points made so far demonstrate that sector ministry is compatible with Methodism's theology of ordination. There is one further criticism that must be faced, though. Some contend that the existence of sector ministry disrupts the unity of the Methodist ministry by creating a class of ministers who are not wholly subject to the discipline of the Conference.

Within Methodism, the notion of ministers being 'in Full Connexion' is of equal importance to ordination. 'Our doctrine . . . is that reception into Full Connexion and ordination are inseparable.'[26] In 1974 the Faith and Order Committee's report 'Ordination' stated that

> Methodism has held to the principle of discipline in a very strong form. 'The Methodist Church recognizes a man's divine call to the ministry, and he himself becomes a Minister, by a process in which Reception into Full Connexion and the Ordination Service are integral parts of the whole' . . . neither is complete without the other.[27]

So what does being 'in Full Connexion' mean? In 1997, the Stationing Review Group said:

> Being 'received into Full Connexion' binds a minister to accept the authority of the Methodist Conference and puts him or her into a formal relationship with the Church's stationing pro-cedures. It also binds the Conference to sustain and support its ministers . . . [It] seals the relationship between a minister and the Conference and binds the two together in a relationship of mutual commitment and obligation.[28]

It has been suggested that

> If a minister is no longer entitled to certain of the privileges of
> Methodist ministers (e.g. housing provision) and if he is freed
> from some of the obligations (e.g. the possibility of immediate
> stationing) it is clear that the term 'Full Connexion' is under
> strain.[29]

It has even been suggested that 'unless a Minister is employed by
the Church he ceases to be a Minister'.[30] Comments such as these
highlight a tension between ordination (which must be under-
pinned by theological reasoning) and being 'in Full Connexion'
which, though undoubtedly of considerable importance within
Methodism, is more a matter of polity than theology. Thus it has
been said that 'There is in our judgment no scriptural or theological reason which requires the ordained ministry to be full
time or to be paid.'[31] Neither is there any scriptural or theological
reason why ministers must be housed by the Church or available
for immediate stationing.

The concept of being 'in Full Connexion' also underlines the
fact that ordained presbyteral ministry is essentially collaborative in nature. It has been said that 'appropriate structures need
to be developed to enable the diverse components of the
ordained ministry to enrich one another, to foster mutual awareness, support and identity'.[32] All sector ministers are stationed
in circuits. They are members of the circuit staff, of the circuit
meeting and of the church council of every church in the circuit.[33]
This is where collaboration must begin. There needs to be a
mutual acceptance and understanding of each other's different
ministries – a willingness to share, a willingness to support and a
willingness to learn. The *structures* are there but ultimately
whether or not collaboration becomes a reality *in fact* depends
on people and not on structures. Indeed, if there is evidence of
sector ministry disrupting the unity of the Methodist ministry
then the cause is more likely to do with personalities than with
principles.

This collaboration is particularly important for sector

ministry. It is part of the process of grounding this ministry firmly within the life of the Church.

It is written in to the whole concept of Sector Ministry that this living link between the Church and the sectors must be firm and strong. Not only does the Church need the sector minister, but the sector minister needs the whole life of the Church, so that his ministry is seen to be in the Church, and in no sense exercised apart from it.[34]

It is necessary 'to establish a clear link between work in a sector and the church as a whole so that the ministry of a [sector minister] may be seen and affirmed by everyone as *ecclesial* ministry'. [35] This has been a constant theme running throughout many of the reports to which we have referred.

It has been agreed by all the various reports produced over the last 30 years that sector ministry *is* a valid expression of ordained presbyteral ministry and, in my judgement, rightly so. All that remains is for us to consider the reality of sector ministry today.

Reality

According to the list of 'Ministers in Sectors and Other Appointments' in the 2000 Minutes of Conference, there were then 108 ministers in sector appointments.[36] To try to get a picture of how things are today, questionnaires were sent to 55 of them.[37] Of these, 37 responded. Questionnaires were also sent to all 33 District Chairs. Of these, 24 responded. It is important to stress that this has not been a structured piece of research but merely a survey of the views of some of the ministers in sector appointments and of those who have ultimate pastoral responsibility for them.

We begin on a positive note. Many of the District Chairs who responded were supportive of the place of sector ministry in the life of the Church. 'The church needs to continue to widen its perspective, to be where people are. It is no longer acceptable to believe that people will come to church. We must go to them.' 'I think it is very important to recognize that the Church's ministry is not just *for* the church, but for the world which is the object of God's love. Sector ministry sends a significant signal about this.' There were also reservations and concerns expressed. We will consider some of them later.

The sector ministers who responded range from people who have been in sector appointments since sector ministry was introduced to those whose experience is limited to a few months. The nature of the appointments covers an equally wide spectrum. Some are highly individualistic – a bus driver, a poet, a story-teller, a sub-postmaster, for example. Others are in what might be called more 'traditional' sectors such as universities, schools and broadcasting.

For most there was a definite sense of call to a particular area of work outside the conventional circuit appointment. 'Whilst studying for the ministry, I started learning and using storytelling to aid my preaching. In a few short months I was literally called (invited) to tell Bible stories all over New England. It felt like a hand other than my own was guiding me towards a special and particular ministry.' 'I became increasingly involved in Retreat work and offering Spiritual Direction. I came to feel that this was the most important thing in my ministry and felt that God was calling me further into it.' 'I had a sense of call to bring together my legal and pastoral training and experience, to represent the Church in an important quest for justice for the individual, and to push out the boundaries of "ministry" as then commonly perceived.'

Such a clear sense of call *into* sector ministry was not the experience of everyone. For some the call was accompanied by feelings of frustration and dissatisfaction with circuit ministry. 'I felt challenged to seek a further development of my ministry, particularly within a Team Ministry. I felt that the Circuit system did not, for me, meet the challenge of the times in which we lived.' Another said he had 'the need to fulfil a side to my calling which is not possible within the Church . . . There was also the need (for me personally) to move on from circuit ministry.'

For one or two the expressed reasons for moving into a sector appointment appear to be wholly negative. One felt '. . . a pro-

this was not uncommon of course

found sense of isolation and futility in the traditional work: isolation from the everyday world, futility at the ministerial routine as traditionally practised – certainly at that time'.

The fact that some ministers move into sector appointments for what, on the surface, appear to be or to include negative reasons, is not of itself crucial. For most people, self-analysis of the motives that lie behind a particular action or decision is rarely a straightforward task. There is frequently a degree of ambiguity even if not readily expressed. Even a strong sense of call to a particular sphere of ministry may, on close analysis, prove to be a predominant rather than an exclusive motive. What is crucial is that the move by *this* minister into *this* sector appointment is judged by *the church* to be right.[38]

This is also the key to one of the concerns expressed by District Chairs. One, though supporting the principle of sector ministry, added that 'At the same time, I would want to see appointments justified as in some sense ministries of word, sacrament and pastoral care, otherwise I cannot see why a *presbyter* should undertake them.' The answer to this concern is surely a matter for the church and not for the minister. Whilst it may frequently be the minister who initiates discussion about a move into a sector appointment, as a matter of discipline and good order it is the church that must decide whether to authorize that move. The criteria for arriving at that decision are clearly set out in SO 743(1). There will be occasions when, as a matter of integrity, the church will have to say 'no'.

Amongst both sector ministers and District Chairs there is a perception of a sector minister as a 'bridge person'. One sector minister said: 'My calling was to be a bridge person – an ordained theologian working in a secular university.' A District Chair observed that 'Sector ministers are a bridge between Church and world.' A bridge must be supported at *both* ends. That observation is trite yet vitally important. For sector ministry to be both effective and consistent with the Church's theology of ordained ministry, a sector minister must have one foot in the Church as well as having one foot in the world. This raises a second area of difficulty. The responses to the questionnaire disclose some concern about the support available to sector ministers.

Firstly, there is concern about the support from the connexion. Some of those who responded felt that the connexion had been very fair to them. Others felt differently. 'The connexion has paid no attention to me.' 'The whole question of the extent to which Methodism "owns" our work seems to me to be one of the major questions. Are we *authorized* to carry out this form of ministry . . . or *given permission*? There is a real difference, if not in practice, at least in the way one feels about one's relationship to the church.' *It would be both*

We noted earlier that when sector ministry was first introduced the Conference appointed a Committee for Ministry in the Sectors with a full-time secretary. Today the equivalent post is only part-time. The shrinking of the post has inevitably had an impact on the level of contact between the connexion and individual ministers. One sector minister observes that 'the decline and fall of sector ministry (at least historically) can be seen in the decline and fall of its pastoral oversight. First there was a full-time overseer . . . then part-time person, then a superintendent minister and then a connexional officer (with many other responsibilities)! All this underlined the fact that Methodism never really knew how to integrate sectors into the church structures.' *lack of personal 5 money!*

Secondly, there is concern about the level of support in the circuits. All sector ministers are stationed in a circuit. Some report that they are both accepted and well used within the circuit, but that is not everyone's experience. One says: 'I was never included in any staff meetings'. Another said that her Superintendent commented that she was 'not one of the working staff'.

The problem also manifests itself in the availability of opportunities to play an appropriate part (i.e. appropriate to the role of a presbyter) within the life of the circuit. 'Three times I've offered to take pastoral charge, but it came to nothing. So my circuit contribution has been largely confined to preaching.' 'I have no role in the local circuit . . . I am largely ignored by the circuit . . .

I am willing to do some preaching and have offered to do one or two things, without much response.' 'I have felt underused throughout my ministry simply because circuits are not structured to cope with people like me. They do not know what to offer us to do once we have exhausted women's meetings and education committees.' *Give the other side Now!*

This must be put in balance. When asked the reasons why some sector ministers were not involved in the life of the local circuit, one District Chair said: 'I would like to know in some cases!' Another said that 'in one case the minister has a rather marginal relationship to the church'. Yet another expressed the view that so far as some sector ministers are concerned it is the case that 'in practice they have left the church'. If this last comment appears a harsh judgement it must be said that more than one sector minister admitted to having become somewhat 'semi-detached'.

The idea of 'connexion' is at the very heart of Methodism. For an ordained minister, being 'in Full Connexion' must surely be more than a matter of polity. It must also become a matter of *experience*. A sense of 'belonging' is crucial to the concept of 'connexion'. When the sense of 'belonging' is weakened it is likely to lead to a feeling of being 'disconnected'.[39] Even small things can trigger intense feelings of being 'disconnected'. 'I think there are significant markers for being a minister. One is the sense of belonging that is affirmed when the Minutes of Conference are both published and issued. That annual sense of exclusion, because I no longer get one and so have no sense of connection to other ministers . . . still hurts every September.' The responsibility for providing ministers with the Minutes of Conference rests with the circuits in which they are stationed.

All of this indicates the need for great care to be taken in the stationing process. Whilst the connexion must determine an application to move into a sector appointment in accordance with SO 743(1), it is also important for consideration to be given to the 'church' end of the appointment – i.e. to the circuit where the minister is to be stationed. It is surely appropriate for steps to be taken at the outset to try to ensure that the minister will be accepted and welcomed in the circuit and that the circuit is willing to 'own' the work that the sector minister has been called to. The role of the Superintendent is particularly important in this process. When stationing probationers the Stationing Committee is required to 'seek to have all ministerial and diaconal probationers stationed in situations where due care and oversight can be given . . .'[40] Perhaps some similar requirement should be introduced to deal with the stationing of those in sector and other appointments.

Thirdly, there is concern about the support of lay people. Amongst the laity there appears to be a widespread lack of understanding – of knowledge even – of what sector ministry is. 'Lay people often asked me why I've left the ministry.' 'Sorry you have left the ministry.' 'Oh, you're not a proper minister then?' When sector ministers were asked what they perceived to be the main criticisms of sector ministry prevalent within the Church the replies were varied. 'It is not a significant ministry.' 'It is seen as a cop-out of "real" ministry.' 'That it is not a proper ministry and is therefore a waste of resources.' 'That those who are trained (expensively) for ministry are not exercising that ministry.' 'A "proper" ministry is to look after a congregation. Otherwise you have deserted the church.' 'I think the Church and individuals within it find it very hard that sector ministers are not part of the stationing process. This is based on a presumption that circuits should have the first call on all presbyters and criticisms are in this area – e.g. they don't accept the discipline of the church; in times of shortage we shouldn't have sector ministers.'

Bearing in mind the fact that it is now more than 30 years since sector ministry was introduced, if the views just set out are at all representative of the general views of the wider church then the difficulties facing sector ministry are stark. Although, at connexional level, there are those making the point that we need to move away from the 'dead hand' of maintenance ministry in the neighbourhood church,[41] it is plain that that message is either not filtering down to, or not being accepted by, the local church. For many of those at the grass roots it would appear that 'preservation' is of greater concern than 'innovation'.

Lot about not much experience 63 yet.

It may perhaps be appropriate to share some of my own experience. When I began ordination training in 1996 my expectation was that I would become a minister in local appointment. It was not until part-way through my training that it was suggested to me that a sector appointment might be more fitting. My secular employment is as a full-time District Judge. The court where I work is situated alongside Leeds Methodist Mission. It was agreed that I should be re-designated as a sector minister to be based at Leeds Methodist Mission but stationed in the Chesterfield Circuit where I live. The different attitudes to sector ministry set out earlier are illustrated, to some extent, by the way people respond to me in these two very different places.

Here we go!

In Leeds it was intended that I should be a bridge between the church and the court. In a variety of ways, some very visible, others less so, this is happening. The folk at Leeds Methodist Mission know what I am doing. They see it as part of a vision they have long held. They have welcomed, encouraged and supported the work I am doing. How many of them knew what a sector minister was when I began I do not know. But they know now! *They have had many Experiment!!! — they even had me!*

L₁?

In Chesterfield it is rather different. Most of my preaching appointments are on the Chesterfield plan – as they were when I was a local preacher. I attend some meetings in Chesterfield but, because of my secular work commitments, my availability is limited. There is little opportunity for me to feed back my experiences 'in the world'. When I tell lay people in Chesterfield that I am a 'sector minister' there is normally a look of bemused indifference. They do not understand. Why should they? The sector I work in is 50 miles away in Leeds. I have no doubt that, if asked, some there would say that what I am doing is a 'cop-out' from 'proper' ministry. *WHY do we have to denigrate people.?*

The preparation of this chapter has been part of my journey of understanding the role of ordained presbyteral ministry in the life of the Church and, within that, of considering whether sector ministry (still) has a meaningful part to play. Once again I let others answer. One sector minister says: 'I believe sector ministry is a sign to the church that God's presence and concern is throughout the world and for all people. It is important that there are those who can point to the sacred within the secular. The church's mission often seems to be about gathering people in rather than being "out there" with them. I would want to affirm other images of mission e.g. . . . showing solidarity and partnership with those outside of the church who are struggling for Kingdom values.' Or, as a District Chair put it, 'The presence of the ordained minister, as long as others in the workplace know the person is ordained, can, as someone said: *Keep the rumour of God alive.*'

Conclusion

At the beginning I indicated that my purpose in writing this chapter was to consider whether sector ministry remains a matter of controversy and resentment today or whether it has now become accepted as a valid form of ordained ministry. At the end of this survey my judgement is that though sector ministry is not as controversial today as it was in the early days, that is largely because many people at the grass roots have no knowledge or understanding – or, perhaps more importantly, experience – of it. It is now more a matter of indifference than controversy. As a result, it has become marginalized.

When it began, sector ministry was a groundbreaking initiative in the search for new and flexible patterns of ministry. Has that initiative now run its course? I do not believe so. There is still an acceptance today (by some, at least) of the importance of presbyters 'being released for more imaginative ways to serve this age'.[42] The Methodist Church must heed the warning given over 40 years ago by Revd Dr Eric W. Baker, then President of the Conference, that 'the danger that may lurk in bold experiments is nothing like so serious as the certain disaster if we don't experiment'.[43] There is an urgent need today for the Church to consider creatively and imaginatively how the whole body of presbyteral ministers can best be used to enable the Church 'to be a sign, a foretaste and instrument of the kingdom'[44] in the twenty-first century.

5

Priests and Prophets but not Servants:
The Presbyterate between the Body of Christ and the Reign of God

Clive Marsh

British Methodists currently know what a deacon is, but not what a presbyter is. This state of affairs may not, admittedly, be reflected at local church and circuit level, especially given the relatively low number of deacons in British Methodism just now. People may not, in other words, know what either a deacon *or* a presbyter is supposed to be and do. But as far as available official statements are concerned, the matter is simple: greater clarity has been offered about the role of the deacon.[1] This observation constitutes the first of two introductory comments I want to make: I do not see any other first step being possible towards an answer to the question 'what is a presbyter?' than to offer the response 'not a deacon'.

Second, I want us to note how important in practical terms the question 'what is a presbyter?' actually is. My first year in the post of Faith and Order Committee Secretary in the British Methodist Church found me encountering the question from many angles. The dominant way in which the question was framed resulted from people's recognition that whilst we all *assumed* we knew what a presbyter is and does, in fact we might not. The sheer scale of tasks we expect of a 'minister', and the range of expectations which churches place upon their presbyter, conspire together to counter the view that a past statement on ordination[2] or the text of the service 'The Ordination of Presbyters, Usually Called Ministers'[3] are sufficient to make clear

[handwritten margin note:] People do Not :- My experience ever call us ' presbyters': No one has ever called us this!

to all what is entailed in being a presbyter. Of course, I do not hear the question 'what is a presbyter?' uttered at all in this form in the context of my local involvement in Methodism. But that does not mean it is not a pressing matter. Everyone knows what their 'minister' should be doing, especially when it is clear that they are not doing what *we* think they should be doing. It is precisely because of this often debilitating, very concrete pressure point – the local practice of, and demands upon, presbyters – that this is a vital question. We need, therefore, to find a theologically informed answer to this question which is workable in practice, even if not one which is simply driven by practice or by the pragmatic requirements of current needs and desires. We shall then need to take responsibility for presenting the results, in all their profound connectedness with the most practical and everyday aspects of how local churches and circuits work, in the widest possible way throughout the Church. It is all very well deciding what a presbyter should be and do. But the Church collectively has to own the results and implement them.

In this chapter, I want to do two things. Accepting and making constructive use of our place within the Protestant critique of how theological authority operates within Christianity I want, first, to explore the dynamic and creative tension between the Church and the kingdom of God. I shall then, second, use this as a framework within which to tease out the role of the presbyter. In other words, I want us to be unreservedly centred on the reign of God (rather than the Church) in our efforts to be theocentric in our theology and practice, and to work out what this means for ministry. In adopting this strategy, I am contending that this is the specifically Christian way of being theocentric. As the American Methodist John Cobb Jr rightly said, theocentrism and Christocentrism are not to be polarized. In Christianity Christocentrism *is* theocentrism.[4]

Christians who stand consciously in the wake of the sixteenth-century European Reformation put the figure of Jesus Christ at the centre of their theological reflection and practice. This is their way of getting their head round what it means to 'put God first' or to stress 'the sovereignty of God' in thought and life. To tease out a Christ-centred approach to ministry will not, though, mean simply focusing upon Eucharist, or focusing upon the teaching of Jesus about the kingdom of God, or finding everything subsumed under an infinitely-stretchable notion of servanthood. It will entail re-conceiving what it means to speak of the presence of God in Christ at different moments, and in different social locations of human life. Locating the presence of Christ in the world will not even mean identifying the Body of Christ too readily with the Church as we know it. As the history of Protestantism's entanglement with the development of Western culture over the past five centuries shows, we are to speak of 'church' as a particular form of human community only in the light of a Christ-centred, kingdom-focused approach to our thought and practice. At its simplest my argument is this: if presbyters are not deacons, then it is the *laity* who are the most focused upon the reign of God in the world, the *presbyters* who are to be focused upon the Church, on the reign of God within the Church and on the Church's mission to the world, and the *deacons* who are to be a hinge, or go-between, between those two, as servants of Christ in the world, and intercessors in the Church. *This sounds fine but is actually pious Nonsense of the church.*

Church and Kingdom in Protestant Understanding

Let me, though, first, set up the dynamic within systematic theology, out of which my concrete suggestions will arise. 'Reformation theology', declared Paul Avis back in 1981, 'is largely dominated by two questions: "How can I obtain a gracious God?" and "Where can I find the true Church?"'[5] Given where Christianity has moved to, and Protestantism in particular, since the Reformation, we forget those primary questions at our peril. To ask a question about God in Europe in the early sixteenth century was inevitably to ask, more directly than is the case today, a question about church. It would be two, even three, more centuries before the Church would begin its shift towards the comparatively weak social and cultural position it holds in the West today. But looking back from our present vantage

??

*The scientific Revolution
the Enlightenment
the French Revolution.*

point, we can see that the Reformation opened up an important conceptual space between church and kingdom, putting the Church firmly in its limited place within the purposes of God. In the process Christians first, and humanity as a whole second, were reminded that God works where God wants to work, and not where humans think God works.

Of course, Reformation emphasis upon the sovereignty of God did indeed put the emphasis on the workings of God being located where God chooses to work. It just so happens that this was more closely tied to the identifiable Church than we might now conclude. But the shift in authority away from the Roman leadership of the Church in the West brought with it substantial re-focusing, re-visioning and even re-branding of Christianity.[6]

The kingdom, or reign, of God as a concept has a chequered past. It is not true to say that the conceptual space opened up between church and kingdom was worked through immediately by the early Reformers. Luther plugged away at a doctrine of two kingdoms – the success of which is open to debate.[7] Arguably he forced religion and politics (i.e. the whole of this world) apart in an unhelpful way as a result. Calvin's *Institutes* scarcely mention the term 'kingdom', and for him it is largely a future eschatological term, even if there is a link with the present preparation which is under way through the agency of God's Spirit.[8] A glance at a batch of recent expositions of John Wesley's theology suggests that the kingdom of God as a concept was not a preoccupation for him either. Furthermore, a 1771 letter finds him stressing that the kingdom of God is an *inner* reality.[9] It may thus be tied in his thinking exclusively to the nature and quality of faith of the believing individual. Reference to some of the giants of the past for support for use of the 'kingdom' in the way that much recent theological discussion has used it, then, is not promising.

As an active concept, though, the kingdom of God does have an important more recent history.[10] Its modern rediscovery is thanks to the philosopher Immanuel Kant. Its reinterpretation and the evolution of its use in a variety of different ways then has a history through Schleiermacher, Rothe and Ritschl, becoming at times all too synonymous with 'the highest common good'. But at least an ethical aspect to it was being rediscovered and accentuated. Johannes Weiss burst the liberal bubble by reminding interpreters that the kingdom of God, for Jesus at least, was not a concept about human ethical endeavours, but a future reality, the coming of which was up to God. At the same time the radical Baptist Walter Rauschenbusch was taking up the liberal interpretation and re-minting it in the context of inner-city New York. More recent developments in the concept's history owe more to liberation movements than to liberalism, and to Roman Catholics than to Protestants.[11] But this may simply be further evidence that in the present some of the best Protestants are Roman Catholic.

I have yet to see the question fully explored, but it may be no accident that the rediscovery and exploration of the concept of the kingdom of God coincides with the numerical and cultural decline of Christianity in the West. When it looks as though God is not around as much as God was in the past, then God is sought both outside the identifiable Church and in God's coming to us from the future.

Now that could, of course, be to turn matters into quite a cynical reading of the way things have developed. But it need not be. It is a very logical development in the history of Protestant theology. *There is a dangerously subversive and even destructively secularizing strand within Protestantism which I do not think we have even yet come to terms with.* At the moment we are still reeling from the social, cultural and political impact of that strand. We have not yet fully worked through its religious and theological implications. But if Christians really are first and foremost to be Christians in the world, and church is but a communal base out of which they do that, then this should be the primary way in which we do our theological reflection, and in which we shape our individual and communal Christian lives. First there is God, then there is world, then there is kingdom, and only then church.

The biggest challenge to Christianity *from within* is its tendency always to be church-centred in the way it does its thinking and acting. But if Christ-centredness, as the Christian form of God-centredness in a post-Reformation secularized Western world, entails being reign-of-God-, rather than church-centred, then our resulting thinking about God, church and ministry has to be shaped accordingly.

Towards a Tense Understanding of the Presbyterate in Methodism

At this point I must turn from the opening up of the tense relationship between the Church and the reign of God – which I am suggesting has become a key systematic theological motif in Protestantism – and ask how we should use this motif for our understanding of ministry, and of the presbyterate in particular, in Methodism. We have brought one consequence of this tension forward from the previous section: Protestantism's support of secularization. A further consequence needs highlighting before we see what happens to ministry.

I recently witnessed a discussion about the way in which screen culture has contributed to the development of individualism in Western culture. One aspect of the debate was whether or not this can be regarded as a continued feature of the Reformation. In contrast to the more common view of the Reformation as a contributor to Western individualism, one contributor argued that the Reformation in fact provided a counter-movement to a tendency to permit priests around Europe to do their own thing in a rather individualistic, idiosyncratic way. The Reformation, by contrast, required people to get back to the source, to orthodoxy and to a common faith. Whilst there is surely more than a grain of truth here about what the Reformation was aspiring to do, I do not think ensuing history bears out this contention as far as the *effects* are concerned. There seems to me little doubt that the Reformation contributed to the development of the processes of secularization *and* individualism, both of which accelerated profoundly with and beyond the Enlightenment.

Now these are sweeping generalizations about the Reformation, secularization and individualism. But it is important that we recognize them (as well as the fact that qualifications and nuances can be added) as we begin to consider the effects of these major cultural shifts upon Christian ministry. With the framework of church and kingdom in place, and the recognition of secularization and individualism as two main consequences of the Reformation, I now want to draw out four observations about the presbyterate in Methodism.

In the first place, if we are, in Methodism, children of the Reformation, then we are heirs to that tendency towards individualism, in both faith and ministry. I do not want to make any lazy value judgement about that; I simply want to note it. Whatever their profound relationship to the body called 'church', presbyters are going to be individual ministers on the basis of the way that thinking has developed within Protestantism and within the Western culture of which we are a part. Furthermore, even allowing for the 'social holiness' emphasis within Methodism, the work of the presbyter as an individual is likely to be construed as work undertaken in relation to other individuals.

Second, the shift in emergent Protestantism away from the authority of the Church to a desire and attempt to focus upon the sovereignty of God opens up the way for *many churches* to exist. If you are basically asking 'where is a gracious God to be found?' and you assume that the answer to that will be 'in some church or other, but which one?', and you disagree that the then culturally dominant form of church is the place where you will find that gracious God, then another will emerge, even if you do not want it to. This has faced all Reformers, and the question rightly appears again and again in church history. Barth and Bonhoeffer faced it head on in a new form in the 1930s and 1940s. The proliferation of churches and the so-called fragmentation of Christianity becomes an easy target for critics of Protestantism. But its cause and source – in the repeatedly asked question of where the gracious God is to be found – needs respecting.

However, to keep on asking where a gracious God is to be found when the Church has grown weak, and when the reign of God has needed to be rethought, leads us to rethink the Church too. The multiplicity of churches is not in itself a bad thing. But if it is accompanied by the sense that each and every Christian can have his or her own denomination, in some ways the logical conclusion of individualism, then we know that this is individualism run riot. Respect for the inevitably communal dimension of Christianity, undoubtedly needed in an individualistic age, may not, however, simply take us towards the revitalization of the churches as we know them. *What if attention to the communal dimension of Christianity is not comprehensively answered by reference to 'church'?* That is a bigger discussion than we can go into here. But it should press us to identify what *forms* of community are appropriate in Christianity.

My second point, then, is essentially this: whilst being heirs of the Reformation we too, in Methodism, are part of the struggle against the individualism to which the Reformation has contributed. We are to respect Christian individuality and personal faith, but we know full well that there is no such thing as the solitary Christian. As far as the presbyter is concerned – given the understandable but dangerous proliferation of churches and Christian groups – this means that we have to identify the primary communal contexts in which we should expect to find a presbyter at work.

Third, whilst it is easy to express the shift in understanding of theological authority which the Reformation brought as a shift from human, ecclesiastical authority to the sovereignty of God, this needs much more unpacking. If you are not to trust and follow the Pope and his representatives, then whom do you trust and follow? Again, the obvious answer – you trust the Bible – proves much too simple. The history of biblical interpretation since the Reformation, and exaggeratedly so in the past two centuries, raises sharply the question whose biblical interpretation you trust: the priests', the scholars', or your own? As far as the presbyterate is concerned, all that has happened is that, by and large, the control of interpretation has simply been seized by, or handed back to, those occupying a priestly order, often for very good reason. But whether Christians in the Protestant tradition have always fully respected this, in a way which enables

their priests/presbyters/ministers/pastors to function as anything
more than mini-popes, is a moot point. In Methodism, we have
to be very precise: we have to explore the question of the extent
to which and ways in which presbyters see interpretation of
Scripture and the traditions of the Church as one of their primary
tasks.

Fourth, we need to note the way that the role of presbyters has
already evolved in the wake of Protestantism's impact on church
and culture. Whatever we might like to think, presbyters are
already doing more than simply serving churches. They are
servants of the state (through handling weddings and funerals) as
well as *servants of the Body of Christ*, which, through the
practice of baptism, is always much bigger than the Church as we
know it. Attention to the sovereignty of God, and to the kingdom
of God, in the context of the secularization of Western culture
has, in other words, already shifted the focus of the presbyterate
away from the easily identifiable form of the Church. A crucial
question for us has to be whether we are happy with all aspects
of this development. Switching that debate into the more conventional terms in which we usually discuss ministry: it has
required our presbyters to be *deacons* through the extent to
which they operate beyond the Church, *prophets* due to the
extent to which they have ended up doing the work of the laity
(as the laity tend to be too narrowly religious for their own and
the Church's good), even whilst the main demands made upon
them are to be *chaplains* to a gathered community of Christians
(or, in some cases, simply to the dying – a task not confined to
hospice chaplains), *administrators* for the church of which they
are a part, and *bureaucrats* for the state in which they serve.

This unreasonable ragbag of responsibilities and roles which
in practice ends up constituting 'the presbyterate' is not merely a
result of ecclesiastical mismanagement, however sluggish
churches may have been in responding in detail to a changing
culture. It is a situation in part caused initially by the Church (in
its post-Reformation forms) and then in part by the social structures resulting from those major changes.

In many ways we may say that it is right and proper that the presbyterate should have evolved in this way in so far as it respects the Church's decline, the tense relationship of church and reign of God, and the need for church to be engaged in mission in the world. The crunch question, though, is why all of these roles have to be required of the presbyterate. If ministry really is dispersed and to be shared throughout the people of God, *as* church and *in* the world, then we have to limit the range of roles and tasks which we expect the presbyter to fill and do. This would not be simple realism and pragmatism. It would be good theology.

Five Marks of the Presbyter

I move, then, from a presentation of a basic, tense framework (church versus kingdom) within which I am contending we should locate our discussions about ministry, and from the highlighting of four crucial markers created by Protestantism's place in the history of church and culture in the West, to some very concrete conclusions as to what a presbyter is, i.e. what a presbyter needs to be in Methodism today.

I begin at a perhaps surprising point. There are not many times when I find myself agreeing with Radical Orthodoxy. But I am compelled to conclude that one of the best developments in our understanding of the presbyterate in Methodism would be to accept that it should become more religious than it currently is. I need to define terms carefully. By 'more religious' I simply mean that presbyters need to accept their limited task to be propounding a particular religious view of life, to be (i) helping to sustain the communities in which that religious view of life is shared, promoted and lived, and (ii) enabling others to be themselves religious in the world outside. I only want to present and promote this notion of a limited, more religious view of the presbyterate, however, in the light of what I have said earlier, i.e. the acceptance of the radically secularized world in which we live, and the unrealistically expanded brief of the presbyter in the contemporary society. It is time to let presbyters be presbyters, and to ensure that other ministries and callings play their full part. That it is *not* happening is not the fault of ordained or lay alone. That it *needs* to happen is the responsibility of lay and ordained alike.

Sensitive ears will hear, behind my reference to Radical Orthodoxy, a more fundamental debt. That is to post-liberalism. My account of Protestantism's contribution to Western culture, and my acceptance of the secularization of society could have been construed and heard in a 1960s or 1970s way, as if I simply espouse a so-called secular theology, and you may have expected me to repeat calls for presbyters to be prophets, or social workers; far from it. Post-liberalism has taught us that there is no such thing as secular theology. Theology can only be done in relation to particular religious communities. Post-liberalism errs in leaving ill explored how those communities talk to each other and the wider world. And it is too prone to imply that religions can be ghettos and that's OK. That I believe that to be disastrous both for religion and society means I can only be a post-liberal liberal. Presbyters do not have to be prophets or social workers. Some people need to be prophets, and some certainly need to be social workers. But those same people do not have to be presbyters. Presbyters need to do something more fundamental. *They need to keep the religion itself going.* They are not alone in doing this. But they alone have this as their primary task.

With this more religious requirement of the presbyter in mind, we can conclude that they must do five things.

They must be theologians

If the Reformation has shifted understandings of authority, then it has put a dangerous amount into the lap of the presbyter. But there is no escaping that responsibility. 'Theologians' may, of course, be the wrong word. Every Christian is a theologian, and that is not the sense I am using it in here. And not every presbyter is a theologian in the sense of being an academic or a scholar. What I mean, of course, is that every presbyter has to be an interpreter of the Bible, a user of the tradition, and an interpreter of the present in the light of Bible and tradition. If they cannot do that, then they cannot model the way that religions actually work, and so they cannot contribute to religion's (in this case, Christianity's) development. *YES*

They must be local guardians of Christian tradition

This is related to the first requirement, but develops it in specific ways. Tradition is always particular, and so a presbyter needs to be very concretely in touch with the particular Christian tradition in which she stands. As such, presbyters are theological resource people. By locality, of course, we may mean region, i.e. circuit. We are not likely in Methodism simply to mean local church, even though a presbyter will carry some responsibility for guardianship in any communal setting she finds herself in. Furthermore, this need not be seen as an exclusive preserve of presbyters, of course. Local preachers share in the local guardianship of the tradition, and how that happens creatively in the collaboration between presbyters, deacons and local preachers must continue to be explored.[12] But guardianship of the tradition is something which a presbyter cannot fail to do.

They must lead worship

If it is true that the church is most the church when it is gathered for worship, then this cannot but be a crucial feature of what a presbyter does. It may seem a bizarre, even heretical, thing to say, but I do think we overplay worship somewhat. It may be true that the church is most the church in worship. But as soon as we make this claim, we tend to put the focus on the *gathered* rather than on the *dispersed* church, and thus on worship in a particular collective, celebratory key. Gathered worship does admittedly have to be high on a presbyter's agenda, though.[13] Again, it is not, and should not be, exclusively the presbyter's task to lead. But presbyters *will* have to lead. This coheres well with the presbyter having a crucial role in the perpetuation of a religious tradition. Worship contributes powerfully to the shaping of religious belief and practice even if it is not everything in a religion, even in Christianity. But Christianity would not be Christianity without worship. So presbyters will lead, and will be major players in the shaping and fashioning of liturgies (in the writing of worship books, for example) and in thinking about new forms of worship.

They must preside at Holy Communion

It has rightly been said that this is the only bit of a presbyter's job that no one else can do. It is mostly true of course. There is the practice of the giving of authorisations to others to preside (the issue about which Faith and Order secretaries appear to receive the most unsolicited enquiries). But despite the number granted, those are exceptions to the rule, the norm. And the norm is a good one. It focuses one order of ministry in a particular way and reminds us that presbyters have as their primary responsibility the task of working with the basic symbols and practices of the religion in which they stand.[14] No one else has presiding at Communion as a central task. The potential significance of presbyters as representatives of Christ may then be developed around this specific task. But it is worth emphasizing that however powerful representation language may prove, it is not a *necessity*. One could appeal just as readily to sociological or socio-psychological rules of thumb in order to maintain a strong sense that it is presbyters, and presbyters alone, who should preside at Communion.

They must be managers of Christian communities

It is under this heading that I include pastoral care, and I use the word managers advisedly. For this acknowledges the structural, organizational skills which will inevitably be required of presbyters if, as part of their primary task, they are responsible for helping people – in this case a community, or set of local communities – to function as a religious group or groups. I am aware there has been quite a lot of discussion in pastoral theology of late as to whether we should see presbyters (priests, vicars,

curates, ministers) as pastors. Presbyters will, of course, require
pastoral skills, given the tasks they undertake and the roles they
must fill. But then all jobs with people do. Seeing ministers
primarily as pastors, though, can contribute to a complex range
of dependencies within the community or communities to which
they relate in a way which may prevent them from fulfilling their
primarily religious task. It can be argued that in order to be
presbyters they must not be pastors. They must co-ordinate the
pastoral care of others. The personal relationships are not necessarily going to be easier, and the presbyter may have to be more
detached than he might ideally like to be. But this may be necessary for the health of both presbyter and community.

Concluding Comments

Those five tasks are, then, I suggest, the primary functions of a
presbyter in the light of addressing the question 'what is a
presbyter?' through the lens provided by the tension between
church and kingdom, as filtered through the development of
Protestantism since the Reformation. I have not begun to address
the question of what kind of person might fulfil these roles. I
have not entered into debates about ontology and function. I do
not want to play down the importance of those debates. What I
have offered is a necessary and appropriately Protestant reading
of the role of a presbyter, arising from the theological drive
which got the whole Protestant thing moving in the first place,
and without which Methodism would not have come into existence. It may well be that the proposal is *too* Reformed for some
and that collectively we shall want to qualify the Protestantism
of the proposal with a dash more Catholic spirit, as would befit
the Methodist tradition. But I offer this as a place to start, as a
way of asking us to respect an important dynamic which comes
from systematic theology, as it has evolved in close interplay
with the development of Western culture.

Rather than ask whether the presbyter is Christ's representative, or represents the Church, I have used Christology
differently. I have sought to ask what happens if, on a Christo-

logical basis, we start with God's reign in the world. I have asked, in effect: if we move from a perspective of God's reign in the world, and then see church and ministry within that, where does it lead? It leads, in my view, to a more limited understanding of the role and functions of the presbyter than has been the case of late.

For the proposal to be sustained, it requires us both to flesh out more fully, and then respect in practice, diaconal and lay ministries. Otherwise what I have taken away from presbyters – the kind of things which would lead many current presbyters to say 'but hold on, you've forgotten x, y and z!' – would not be addressed at all. The real challenge is whether we can achieve a more limited presbyterate, and a more focused and enlivened diaconate and laity, without re-ghettoizing presbyters in the process. I wonder whether we can.

[Handwritten marginal notes:]

Debatch.
Yet.
It is interesting that No one has yet mentioned the Holy Spirit!

I am not at all sure that the distinction is all that important. No doubt a limited view.

6

The Presbyter as President:
Presidency at the Eucharist as the Defining Paradigm of Presbyteral Ministry

RICHARD CLUTTERBUCK

We are urged to make our theology more experiential and contextual. For me that is a hard discipline. I am, as I like to tell my colleagues, a 'recovering existentialist', all too aware of the quicksand that lies in wait for those who stray from the well-trodden path of the Christian tradition. But let me break my own rule and confess that the starting point for this chapter is indeed experiential. The experience is easily described: there is no situation where I have a greater sense of my presbyteral ministry than when I stand at the Lord's Table. It has been the highest privilege of my ministry – in a huge variety of situations – to preside at the Eucharist, particularly when I stretch out my hands to recite the great prayer of thanksgiving. Indeed, my personal reflection on what it means to be a presbyter flows from precisely this point and this experience.

In these reflective moments, I find myself asking questions such as these: Why am I the one who stands behind the table and presides? If I am honest, I know myself to be far from the most spiritual, the most wise, the most holy, or the most competent Christian in the company. What is it, therefore, about my situation and office that makes me the right person for this role? Along with these, is the further question: What is congruent with this eucharistic presidency? In other words, how does my role within, and on behalf of, the Christian community cohere with my role as its eucharistic president?

What follows is essentially a more disciplined reflection on these questions. I hope it will be a worthwhile avenue for exploration. I intend to do my best to avoid the traditional controversies over functional versus ontological understandings of ordained ministry, as well as the debate on the appropriateness of the word 'priest' for the ordained minister. Nevertheless, my own prejudices are more than likely to show through and I will be happy to have them challenged.

Christ, the Community and the Eucharist

Let me begin this exploration by stating the obvious: the Church is the *ecclesia* of Jesus Christ. It is not merely a federation of those who seek to follow his teachings – though I do not want to underplay the importance of that for a moment. Neither is it the sum total of those who acknowledge him as Lord and Saviour – and the importance of that cannot be denied either. But the Church is primarily the body of Christ. By the power of the Holy *at* Spirit the whole body is given gifts and enabled to share in the *last !* mission of God. Yet, from the earliest times, this universal gifting of the Spirit has gone along with gifting focused on particular individuals. But we need to get it in the right order: the risen Christ calls together the community that meets in his name. His spirit animates it. Within it are individuals who are called to serve Christ by serving his Church. As the contemporary Roman Catholic theologian Edward Schillebeeckx writes: 'The Church itself is the womb of ministry, which is itself in the service of the community of believers and draws on its mystical depths.'[1]

I have chosen to use the term 'president' to describe the role of the presbyter. I will try to show that this role links the liturgical office of the presbyter with the other roles that relate to being an ordained person within a Christian community.

'Presidency', it seems to me, is a term with both enough precision to make it meaningful, but enough elasticity not to bind the Church into a particular historical or cultural model of ministry. What theological backing might there be for a presidential understanding of presbyteral ministry? I have already

pointed to a number of sources. In more recent theology I am
indebted to at least three authors. The first is the Orthodox theologian John Zizioulas who, in his influential work *Being as
Communion*,[2] speaks of the way in which the Eucharist is con-
stitutive both for the corporate nature of the Church and for the
personhood of those who share in it. I would not expect a
Methodist audience to share all of Zizioulas's conclusions
(especially, perhaps, his strong Christological backing for
ministerial structures),[3] but I would want to stress three aspects
of his thought that should be congenial to us. First, that the
doctrine of the Trinity provides Christians with their best model
of community – one in which there may be presidency (the
Father), but there is not inequality. Second, that the identity of
persons might best be described in terms of relationality, whether
the personhood is that of a member of the Trinity or a member of
the Church. We become persons through participation in relationships rather than first becoming persons and then entering
into relationships. Third, that the Eucharist is that event which
both represents and constitutes the Church's reality as the spirit-
filled icon of Christ. As one interpreter of Zizioulas puts it, 'the
Eucharist makes the Church'.[4] My second source is Hans Küng –
almost as different a modern theologian as you could imagine.
He has pioneered an attitude towards priesthood that stresses its
integration with the ministry and mission of the whole Christian
community:

> It is precisely when he is really in the Lord's service that he is
> really in the community's service too. Then it can be seen
> clearly that he is acting selflessly, that he is there as a president
> of the community, and that the community is not there for the
> president. For this reason, and expressly in the service of the
> gospel, the president of the community will spare no pains in
> his effort to realize the needs, difficulties and hopes of his
> community.[5]

Elsewhere in the same work, Küng makes an explicit link
between the role of sacramental presidency and presidency in the

life of the community: 'Relying on proclamation, the president also directs the Church by means of the sacraments. He welcomes into the community, assembles it for the eucharistic celebration and presides over it.'[6]

My third example from recent explorations of the notion of ministerial presidency, that of Robin Greenwood (albeit with a strong Church of England cast), is particularly helpful. In *Transforming Priesthood*[7] he suggests that:

> [T]he relation between clergy and laity is adequately expressed when the particular responsibilities of the presbyter are presented in terms of overseeing amongst the other ministries that constitute the local eucharistic community. That concept will . . . be explored in terms of presidency.[8]

Presiding at the Eucharist: Historical and Theological Reflections

As Edward Schillebeeckx pointed out in his work on ministry,[9] the position of the ordained minister in the Christian community, and the theological arguments establishing that position, have changed over two millennia, and have always been to some extent historically contingent. It is important to recognize this, otherwise we tend to fall into one of two errors: either we maintain inflexible adherence to inherited models of ministry, or we hark back to a golden age – in the New Testament period or later – when the Church had got it exactly right. That being said, history and tradition do have some claim on us. We are not, after all, cast adrift on a desert island with a copy of the New Testament and the task of inventing a new religion based on it. Furthermore, history and tradition provide resources for a Church seeking to be faithful in a fast-moving present. Schillebeeckx himself suggested that the models of ministry prevalent in the first millennium can help the Roman Catholic Church overcome some of the problems facing it at the end of the second.

So, with that apology, I briefly turn to the historical tradition of identifying the presidency at the Eucharist with the presbyter. The details of that history, especially the very beginning in the first century, have long been a matter of controversy, and I have no new light to shed. What does seem to be clear, though, is a trajectory along which the relationship between ordained ministry and the community's celebration of the Eucharist developed. Whilst there is no early evidence, in the first and second centuries, that the language of priesthood was applied to presbyters and bishops, there is, according to Bernard Cooke's massive study of the history of Christian ministry,[10] a growing association of the *episkopoi* and *presbyteroi* with liturgical presidency. The understanding of the Eucharist developed alongside, and in relation to, the understanding of ordained ministry. He suggests that the evidence for the early centuries (from, for example, Ignatius, Justin and Hippolytus) leans, if anything, towards the *episkopos* having the prime presidential role. Presbyters could be seen as presiding by delegation from, or alongside, the bishop. I am not going to turn this chapter into an argument for bishops, but this line of thought does suggest that from an early stage the Church associated presidency in the celebration of the Eucharist with oversight in the life of the community. That is a theme to which I hope to come back later.

Presidency at the Eucharist as an Indicator of the Presbyteral Role

At the heart of my argument is the suggestion that the structure of the Eucharist – the service at which the presbyter normally presides – will give us helpful pointers to the question, what is a presbyter? For that reason, I want to take the order for 'Holy Communion during Ordinary Seasons (First Service)' from the *Methodist Worship Book* of 1999. I realize, of course, that the Eucharist is much more than this. It also provides – and perhaps with even greater clarity – answers to the questions, 'what is the ministry of the Church?' and 'what is the vocation of a Christian?' But it is part of the richness of the Eucharist that we can turn to it for a response to so many of the great questions of

Christian life and thought. Incidentally, I hope that the exposition I am giving will also underline why some parts of the service should normally be said or done by the person presiding.[11]

The Gathering of the People of God

The Eucharist is a brief time of gathering for the people of God, who are most commonly scattered in the wider community. The president is responsible for shaping this moment of gathering, indicating by both word and action the welcoming love of God, the purpose for which the congregation has gathered, and the urgent necessity for the confession of sin. As the one responsible for the gathering of the people of God, the presbyter acts as a shepherd, one who calls people to the source of refreshment and challenge. He or she acts as a focus for the communal worshipping life of the Church. As president the presbyter does not create the Church, nor does he or she necessarily lead its people to a new place. But he or she does call them together and remind them who they are. The presbyter is one who reminds God's people both of the duty to be open and honest before God, and of the liberating power of God's forgiveness. It is a presidential role to announce what is happening. That is what the presbyter does in the declaration of God's forgiveness, both in the Eucharist and in the daily exercise of his or her ministry.

The Ministry of the Word

Central to the celebration of the Eucharist is the reading and exposition of the Scriptures. Neither are exclusively presbyteral tasks – though even in Methodism the preacher at the Eucharist is more often than not a presbyter – but the minister does preside at the occasion of their reading and exposition. This presidency suggests that part of the role of the presbyter involves reminding the local church that it is a community under the Word and enabling that community to discern God's Word for that time and place. In the Eucharist the presbyter brings to this task the resources of biblical and doctrinal study, pastoral sensitivity and social awareness. She or he is also called to represent the wider hermeneutic community of the Church. In this way, the Word interpreted and discerned in one time and place is related to the Word interpreted and discerned through the whole historical tradition and through the world-wide catholicity of the Church. There is nothing in this understanding of presidency of the Ministry of the Word that prevents the presbyter acting in a prophetic role, but it does suggest that the presbyter also interprets Scripture and tradition in relation to the community and the context of its cultural setting.

The Prayers of Intercession

This, of course, is another aspect of the Eucharist that is far from being the exclusive preserve of the presbyter. Yet, once again, it is the presbyter who presides at this presentation of lament, concern and pleading. It should be part of the presbyteral role to ensure that the intercessions of a congregation reflect the whole range of human need, and particularly the prayerful solidarity that exists between Christians in different situations. Often as not the day-to-day pastoral ministry of the presbyter and her or his colleagues will both feed into the prayers of intercession, and be redirected by them.

The Peace

This is a moment in the Eucharist that is normally led by the president. It is, of course, not about greeting our friends; rather, it is about reminding us of the kind of community the Church is and is called to be. The presbyter is the one who calls the community to recognize the reconciling presence of Christ, and calls it to reflect the reality that the Eucharist proclaims. The admonitions given by the presbyter in the Book of Common Prayer order for Holy Communion reflect this concern and this vocation. To preside at the Peace also means to take some responsibility for reconciliation within the Church, and for witnessing to the reconciling ministry of Christ outside it.

The Confession of Faith

The Nicene Creed is traditionally the form in which eucharistic congregations affirm their faith to be in continuity with that of the universal Church. It is by no means the sole responsibility of the presbyter to preserve the community from doctrinal error, but the maintenance of sound doctrine – 'believing and preaching our doctrines' – is enshrined in Methodist usage as an important aspect of the presbyter's (especially the Superintendent's) role.

The Prayer of Thanksgiving

Here the president (almost always for Methodists a presbyter) does three things. She or he has the role of authorized storyteller, recounting the glory of the triune God expressed in creation, redemption and consummation. It is a role similar to that exercised by particular people (called *matapulé*) who are responsible for maintaining the language and story of the community in some Pacific Island societies. The presbyter is called to carry the community's story and to make it a present reality. She or he recites, of course, the words of institution, accompanied by the actions of taking, blessing and breaking the bread. I do not want to say that the president stands here as an icon of Christ, but she or he is presiding over and representing the community's call to be the icon of Christ. In the climax of the eucharistic prayer, the *epiclesis*, the president calls upon the Holy Spirit to transform both the bread and wine and the gathered people to become the vehicles of the risen Christ's blessing.

The Blessing and Dismissal

It is traditional that the presidential presbyter pronounces a final blessing, whilst the deacon, if present, dismisses the congregation to the work of being Christ in the world at large. Greenwood, in fact, sees blessing as one of the distinctive marks of a presidential approach to ordained ministry:

A presiding ministry consists largely in encouraging others to see what they are called to and have the gifts for, and then sustaining them as they grow into their ministries . . . within the whole priestly Church of Christ, the ordained minister, perpetually in a relationship of mutuality, presides by exercising a ministry of blessing.[12]

Episkopé *and Types of Presidency*

Clearly, there are a number of different kinds of presidency and many ways of exercising a presidential role. The President of Ireland and the President of the United States, for example, have very different roles. To speak of presidency as the most appropriate designation for presbyteral ministry is not to commit ourselves, in advance, to any one of the many possible forms of presidency available. What it does commit us to is an understanding of presidency which takes its lead from the ministry of Jesus, and which is congruent with the presbyter's role in the celebration of the Eucharist.

In fact, those of us who take on presidential roles do so in a number of different ways. Two examples from my own ministry could illustrate this. I am currently chair of the Executive of the Conference of Anglican and Ecumenical Institutes of Ministerial Training. It is an active role and one that depends on my having some understanding of and competence in the field of ministerial training. It is, though, an essentially servant role, one in which there is both collaborative working with my colleagues on the executive and constitutional limits to actions that we can take. In my previous appointment, I was president of Muswell Hill Methodist Lawn Tennis Club. Here, competence did not come into it. I have a fair idea of how tennis should be played, but neither the inclination, nor the ability, to play it. My presidential role was confined to chairing meetings, sorting out disputes and liaising with other bodies. If people needed to know how to play tennis, they called the coach!

I draw your attention to these apparently trivial examples because it is important to see a presidential presbyterate as compatible with service and collaboration, rather than entailing a commitment to monarchical autonomy. For example, the work on 'Servant Leadership' of the American Quaker businessman Robert Greenleaf has been taken up by a number of Christian traditions with a high view of ordained ministry.[13]

Whilst there are many forms of presidency, all of them involve a degree of oversight. John Wesley is said to have justified his own exercise of oversight of the Methodist Societies, and his eventual ordination of presbyters for work in America, by asserting that there is no clear distinction in the New Testament between *episkopos* and *presbyteros*. In a number of ways contemporary consensus is on his side. Few would now suggest that the New Testament provides a clear blueprint for the threefold ordering of Christian ministry (however much that ordering may have later developed under the guidance of the Spirit). There is also widespread agreement, even in churches with an episcopal model of government, that *episkopé* is not confined to the ministry of one person; it is, to some degree at least, dispersed among other leaders in the community, or resides in the corporate structures of the Church. In the Church of England, for example, there is a frequent slogan that 'every incumbent is a training incumbent', and the suggestion is commonplace that, far from being the one who delivers all Christian ministry in a community, the presbyter oversees, co-ordinates and envisions the ministry of many people in several communities.

This I take to be congruent with the presbyter's role as president at the Eucharist. The service itself, I have argued, points to the way in which the presbyter exercises a presiding role in the community of faith. The Methodist language of 'pastoral charge' picks up much of what I mean by this, though it needs spelling out more clearly. Because the presbyter (who, of course, never acts in isolation from the local or wider Christian community) has a responsibility for discipline and justice, she or he is doing much more as eucharistic president than expressing a relationship of pastoral care.

If the Eucharist is the place where we celebrate what it is to be the Church of the crucified and risen Jesus, then the one who presides has a key role, in enabling the community to explore what it means to live eucharistically – to praise God in mission and service. It is this, I have argued, which is at the heart of presbyteral ministry.

' Clutters' is an old pupil of mine!

7

Collaborative Ministry and the Ministry of the Whole People of God

ESTHER SHREEVE

This chapter is written from the perspective of teaching on an ecumenical ministerial training course, which has students preparing for different kinds of ministry, both ordained and lay, for various churches – predominantly Anglican, but also Methodist, United Reformed, and sometimes Baptist and Roman Catholic. But I write also as the wife of a Methodist minister, with certain convictions which may be perceived as axes to grind by people who do not share them! It is important to come clean at the outset.

One of my passions is to play an active part in encouraging Christians to live out their calling, to develop their gifts, to help them grow in confidence and articulacy, and thus be set free for ministry, in whatever sphere that may be. Of course, this is also one of the responsibilities of an ordained minister, but it is a responsibility which the people of God exercise corporately. In the process it is wonderful to watch people grow spiritually; as their gifts are discovered and recognized, they are given wings and enabled to fly. It is another slant on Hebrews 5.12–14: as disciples learn and are encouraged to put what they are learning into action, they are able to do more and more. If they drank only milk, and never moved on to solid food, they would remain as babies in the faith.

So it was good to be part of the Commendation service we held at the last residential weekend of the course, when we sent our leavers out having commissioned them for ministry. Some were

going to be ordained as deacons in the Church of England, a
couple were starting their intern year with the United Reformed
Church, one Methodist was leaving us, having already done a
year's probation, and a handful of lay students were moving on,
after spending one or two years with us. The same words were
said to each individual: 'Go in peace to love and serve the Lord.'
The traditionalists, or nervous ones, replied simply, 'In the name
of Christ, Amen'. Others were more forthright, coming out with
replies ranging from 'Yes, please!' to 'Hallelujah!' But what was
very moving was to see over 30 people all going out to *minister*
in a wide variety of situations, the course having equipped them
as well as it could. I had the opportunity to speak to them that
weekend about ministry – ministry in the context of being the
other side of the coin of discipleship, the outworking of the faith
and commitment of the *laos*, the people of God. I based much of
what I was saying on recent Methodist reports, particularly
'Called to Love and Praise' (1999):

> The word *laos* hardly ever denotes lay people as different from
> leaders and presbyters. The ministry of the people of God in
> the world is both the primary and the normative ministry of
> the Church, for the Church is as much itself in the world as it
> is in the Church . . . the ministry is expressed in Christ-like
> giving, in social action, and in witness to the Christian gospel
> . . . In Methodism, the ministry of lay people has been essential
> to the very functioning of the church from the start . . . the
> partnership of ordained and lay ministers remains vital to the
> work and well-being of the Church.[1]

Other churches have come to see this in recent years; the Roman
Catholic Church, post Vatican II, has seen some interesting
developments, as Peter McIsaac has pointed out:

> The Second Vatican Council, then, calls the laity to exercise
> their unique ministry in the Church's mission, which comes
> from their privileged place in the world. In the daily labours of
> their working lives, the laity are at the heart of the world

where the Church needs to bring its healing, reconciliation and transformation. But they do not only bring the grace of the Church to the world; they also bring the needs, desires and sufferings of the world into the worship of the Church and before the altar. The unique place of the laity in the world and in the Church recalls powerfully that Christ came to draw the whole world into the loving communion of the Trinity, and it was because of the Father's love of the world that he sent his Son and pours out their Spirit to continue the work of redemption begun in his loving creation.[2]

This is expressed also by Ward and Wild in *Guard the Chaos*, when they comment:

> Much contemporary worship fails to connect with people's experience. . . most church liturgy cannot be said to be a ritual experience of the community's life. Can clergy hand over the creation of liturgy to those whose lives it is supposed to express before God, recognizing that they too will be a part of the group? It is not enough that chosen members of the congregation are given parts in what is still essentially the vicar's play.[3] *They will probably say 'No'!* —

Inevitably, this discussion leads to debate about the role of presbyters and deacons in Methodism. Some of my favourite quotes from 'The Ministry of the People of God' (1988) are: 'The call to ministry can easily be misunderstood to refer only to the calling of an ordained minister';[4] 'Those whom God calls to the ordained ministry cannot expect adequately to fulfil the role, either individually or collectively.'[5] Does this tie in with the imperfect expression of *episkopé* referred to in the report from Conference in 2000?[6] 'Good leadership releases, encourages and facilitates the putting to good use of the enormous variety of gifts among all God's people in the service of the church.'[7]

To help me to think further about ministry, I asked our students to consider how their own gifts were recognized and encouraged, how they could do the same for others, and what

personal and institutional barriers get in the way. They gave me
some very helpful and quite profound answers. With regard to
the recognition of their own gifts, this was how they responded:

- encouragement of others – family, school, work, church etc.
- being allowed to try things without fear of failure
- self-discernment
- self-acceptance
- natural flair encouraged
- right timing
- opportunity provided by an interregnum (something we rarely
  have in Methodism!)
- opportunity for a new minister to come in as a talent scout
  (something we do experience regularly in Methodism!)
- being asked if you realize you are an answer to prayer
- the sheer joy of doing a job you feel called to do
- knowing you don't have to do a job for ever (six-year rule?!)
- the ethos a congregation may have of older people encouraging younger members.

Their observations about recognizing other people's gifts over-
lapped with the above to some extent. But there were fresh
insights too:

- the whole body of the church has an awesome responsibility
  here – to build each other up
- remember that the exercise of gifts promotes spiritual growth
  and maturity
- time is needed to get to know people well enough to discern
- there is a joy in recognizing other people's gifts – like the
  excitement of a teacher spotting a pupil who is basically
  brighter than they are!
- support and training must be given
- be ready to cause turmoil in someone's life
- calling is about something bigger than one's own needs and
  desires
- it is important to help people feel valued and needed

- be aware of the difference between discernment and a management decision
- value 'being' as well as 'doing'.

Their insights into the barriers to the recognition of gifts were honest, and rang bells with everyone who was listening:

- time is of the essence, and there usually is not enough of it – certainly not after a Sunday service
- lack of training for, and commitment to, collaborative ministry
- many tasks appear to be made over-complicated with talk of training
- it is easier and quicker to do it yourself
- making assumptions
- ordained person may want to be in control and laity may want to collude
- it is easy to make people feel guilty
- fears of failure, rejection, conflict etc.
- age of many in congregations may hinder a change in attitude
- apparent barriers – rejection, frailty etc. – may actually be what God wants to work with
- lack of role models.

This last point spoke volumes to me: I am a lay person, fully committed to my work, which I love. But I had to be persuaded by several people to apply for my job in the first place, and met with blank incomprehension, even hostility, from some in my church who simply could not credit that I, a lay person, should be concerned with training ministers. I think many would have felt much happier about my working had I been ordained, because that would 'fit' their view of ministerial training – and also be less threatening to their own view of what it means to be a disciple of Christ, i.e. if you are really *that* keen, you should be ordained. Ouch!

Encapsulated in 'The Ministry of the People of God' is a detailed discussion of how gifts may, or may not, be recognized.

The matching of gifts to individuals, with their tasks in and for the church, is a subtle and sensitive procedure, involving discernment and testing. The following patterns have been evident in the Church throughout its history:

The whole Church, together with the individual concerned, recognizes in a person the gifts needed for a particular piece of work or a long-term task.

The Church recognizes in an individual the gifts and graces needed for a specific ministry; even though those concerned may be unaware of their potential in that area of service, or reluctant to offer themselves for the work required, the Church calls them to fulfil this ministry.

An individual is inspired by the Spirit to initiate a particular project or serve a need; the Church fails at the time to discern the Spirit's work and only belatedly recognizes and honours such a prophetic ministry.[8]

Two things strike me from this. First, the very welcome admission that the Church can, and does, make mistakes. I am sure we all know people we think should, or should not, be doing particular jobs. The joy, and comfort, is that we believe in a God of redemption, who helps us to work with, and through, the mistakes – so that, often, we can eventually see that perhaps it was not even a mistake after all! The second is the implicit recognition of the need for honesty in assessing a church's situation, and allowing the Holy Spirit room to manoeuvre by not papering over the cracks. The way in which churches are encouraged now to conduct regular audits of their situation, as in *Pilgrim's Way*,[9] is a wonderful opportunity for growth and development.

Let us take a look at the word collaborative now – it is the buzzword in ministerial terms, A Good Thing, something to which we should all be aspiring. In 'Lay Presidency at the Lord's Supper' (1984) we read that:

There is a growing realisation that there is but one ministry expressed in a variety of ways and shared between ordained and lay . . . we in Methodism have come to recognize we have been slow in making demands upon and giving responsibility to our lay people, and that the reputation we enjoy in the Church at large for the employment of lay people is largely undeserved. We are now beginning to understand what collaborative ministry means.[10]

What *does* it mean? There are connotations here of co-operating with the enemy (as in Occupied France in the last war). It could be scientists working together on a specific research project. Or else we are talking of agencies, which would not normally have anything to do with each other, actually getting on and doing something constructive. Is this what we want to imply when we talk about being collaborative? It raises all sorts of hilarious images of how clergy, deacons and church members have not loved and respected each other in the past – or even today! Who is the enemy – our colleagues – or the big, bad world out there? Perhaps we should be thinking of mutual or corporate ministry – or even better, miss out the adjective altogether. What we must avoid at all costs is falling into the trap of conniving or colluding or of not confronting issues, so that the *status quo* can be maintained, and congregations left in a blissful, unchallenged and unchallenging state.

As I have already quoted from one of the reports on lay presidency, I want to take the opportunity to pursue this a little further. In the Methodist Church we have the option of authorizing a lay person to preside (an inheritance from the Primitive Methodists), when occasion requires it. We hold this in tension with the view that it should normally be an ordained presbyter who fulfils this role, and in the context of ecumenical dialogue this is a vital issue. As I read the various statements on the question of who should be authorized to preside at the Lord's Table, and consider the current shortage of presbyters, particularly in rural circuits, I want to make a few observations. The Church agrees that we are talking here of Christ's sacrament; the person who is presiding at the Lord's Table is representing Christ to the congregation, and vice versa, who all should feel that they have a part to play in the celebration of the Lord's Supper. So, of course, it is absolutely right that there should be a process of vetting to make sure *as far as possible* that the person who is leading the congregation in the Great Prayer of Thanksgiving will not be an obstacle in the way of people worshipping. But church history is full of instances when questions have arisen over the fitness of someone to do this – for example the Donatist controversy in the fourth century, when some would not accept Communion from the hands of those they considered traitors. We come then full circle – the Church came to the conclusion that the sacrament was not invalid just because the person presiding was seen as being a sinner. What a relief – because who isn't?

Since becoming a member of staff on a ministerial training course I have occasionally been invited to assist with the distribution of Communion at our services. I have to say, I do not have a burning desire to preside, but I have found it an enormous privilege to give students and colleagues, whom I know quite well, the bread or wine. This came as a surprise to me, as I would not regard myself as having a particularly 'high' view of the sacraments, and this is certainly a factor in my belief that I have not been called to ordination. Now I wonder whether I, as one who has not been through a ministerial selection procedure, am placing an obstacle in anyone's way when I help with the distribution of the elements. Would it feel any different if I were to be authorized by the Methodist Conference to assist? I am not suggesting that we need yet another authorization to do something in worship – but I am aware that it may be difficult for some to receive the elements from me on occasion!

Is this not very similar to the role I have as a local preacher? I hope that in what I am saying from the pulpit, I am able to bring people closer to God. That in itself is a humbling and challenging role to have to fulfil, and something I do not do lightly. Methodism has always taken the preaching of the Word very seriously; hence we have to qualify as local preachers before we are let loose on our congregations. But I would argue that there is more room for distortion of the gospel in the pulpit being open to those who are not authorized to preach, than there is in a

There is a muddled argument here I fear.

Communion service being led by someone who is not ordained. In Methodism we do, of course, try to protect the pulpit, in that only those whom the Superintendent minister approves may preach – but I wonder how many invited preachers the Superintendent actually knows. We can all, I am sure, produce horror stories of disastrous sermons we have heard, preached by clergy, local preachers, and lay people who have been specially invited. With the trend towards using set services, and more particularly the *Methodist Worship Book*, the scope for disaster in a Communion service is comparatively small, although even this can be abused by a non-liturgically minded person, irrespective of whether they are ordained or not!

It seems to me that we have an opportunity here to review, and then perhaps reaffirm, what message we are giving to people about ministry when we authorize someone to preside at Communion. Ministry has to be rooted in the *laos*, the whole people of God. In 'The Sunday Service; the Great Prayer of Thanksgiving' (1990) we are told:

> Active participation in worship, both by the entire gathered company and by individuals and groups within it, is highly desirable. The president should lead the Great Prayer, fulfilling a vital symbolic role, and should further exercise a leading role throughout the service. But he or she need not and should not do everything . . . Lay people should be given ample opportunity . . . to administer, to lead intercessions, to read lessons, to preach . . . The whole congregation celebrates the Lord's Supper.[11]

Hence it is logical to argue that in cases of possible deprivation, it should be possible for the *laos*, a particular congregation, or circuit, to identify someone whom they would like to recognize as authorized for a specific period of time to preside, and this authorization be approved by Conference. After 16 years of life in rural circuits, I have only experienced one period when it was necessary to ask for an authorization for someone other than the minister to preside, and that was when my husband's colleague

This is the vital element. (Like the Pope giving permission No!) Just Bill Kelly! – who approved of it.

was taken ill, and there were 21 chapels to cover. The call, when it is made, should come from the people of God; it could be for a respected member of the people to take that role, when no minister could be there. But there should be a clear understanding that the call is not something that the individual is seeking for him or herself. In fact, it is more than likely that they will be unwilling to do it, reluctant because of feelings of total unworthiness.[12] This is very close to the situation we have at present; but it appears that the practice of allowing dispensations for someone who is not ordained to preside varies widely from district to district, and is, in the vast majority of cases, usually restricted to probationers, lay workers, or deacons. I wonder if we should not also be looking at the possibility of a steward, pastoral visitor, local preacher or loved and respected member of the congregation being authorized, *if* the context requires it. This view was endorsed by a couple of members from the Authorizations Committee, when I asked them how authorizations were distributed. I was told that there had been, in recent years, a couple of requests for ministerial wives to be authorized; that a few circuits had had the vision of an authorization being given to someone for three years, and then being given to someone else, if still required. But the general practice has been for people already in recognized ministry, deacons, lay workers, and, of course, probationers, to be named recipients of authorizations. One friend observed that in a circuit where he had been a minister, he had tried hard to persuade the church stewards that they could conduct a baptism if he could not be there. How sensible, when one considers how baptisms can stockpile, waiting for a ministerial appointment, so that almost all the services a minister may take in a particular church contain a baptism or two! But, although they agreed reluctantly that they might be willing to do the odd one, they made sure that it never happened!

What we must avoid, at all costs, is the idea of 'cheap' or 'second class' ordination, where people are ordained, simply to get around the problem of having sufficient Communion services. I confess that I do have some reservations about the way our category of Minister in Local Appointment (non-stipendiary minister, who is not itinerant) can be viewed, for that very reason; we have a big education exercise on our hands to demonstrate that this is *not* what being an MLA is about. But that is another discussion which needs to happen.

This is not a call for blanket authorizations for lay presidency. I am not suggesting that the role of minister of Word and Sacrament be taken away from the presbyter. Far from it. What I am advocating is that this be seen in a much wider context, and does not necessarily mean a clerical monopoly of presiding at the Lord's Table, if circumstances demand it. What is actually a much more demanding and all-encompassing role is that of helping a congregation or circuit to *live as a eucharistic community*, or indeed as the community of the baptized. That seems to me to be one of the key roles of presbyters: they are in a position to lead, guide, enable, facilitate, and even discipline when required – in fact, to provide some degree of oversight – that word *episkopé* again. They are people who can provide much of the vision and perspective with regard to what it actually means to a congregation to live out from day to day the participation in the Lord's Supper which they have celebrated on Sunday. The strands of eucharistic theology are many and varied – including sacrifice, reconciliation, forgiveness, nourishment, remembrance, sharing, celebration. Are these not all part of our lives of discipleship which we are called to live as members of the Body of Christ? And is it not infinitely more difficult and challenging to help a church to live the eucharistic life, than to represent Christ to the congregation through presiding at Communion? Of course, it is not the responsibility of the presbyters alone to do this, but surely the fact of their ordination implies that they have a particular contribution to make here.

A story from my own experience was of a church where there was a split over an issue which really got the congregation wound up. Acrimony was the dominant emotion. The minister refused to take a Communion service there until the problem was sorted out. The result was that a group of the congregation left that church, and the congregation was then able to move forward again. I wonder how many ministers have that sort of confidence and courage? Part of the role of the presbyter, in particular, is to risk being made scapegoat from time to time – there is a theological point to be made here, linking the priestly and the sacrificial role, although I would not want to make too much of it as this, I think, is something which is part of the cost of discipleship generally. This is not popular language these days when we have, rightly, made huge steps forward in establishing that neither the presbyter, nor the family of the manse, should be put on a pedestal, and be the focus of unrealistic expectations. But there will be times when she or he will have to take the flak, no matter how unfair or undeserved it may be, simply because of the fact of her or his ordination.

This brings us back to the question of how the presbyter is going to exercise her or his leadership and authority. It is easy to understand why there has been a temptation to do it all oneself; if the buck stops with the minister, who is the 'named', or representative person, it might feel safer to try to do it all oneself, even if one is not omnicompetent. But that is doing no favour at all to fellow Christians. What about the responsibility ministers have to recognize and encourage other people's gifts, and to help them to develop as mature Christians, used to strong meat? Delegating, or even more radical, *handing over* responsibility, is a risky business. It requires maturity, generosity of spirit, and above all, grace. And the hard graft of working out how one is going to exercise one's ministry should surely be done collaboratively, taking the views and vision of other members of the people of God into account.

We live in an imperfect world. God's Kingdom is partly here, and we await its fulfilment, when Christ comes again. Meanwhile, we have to keep on keeping on, constantly on the move, trying hard to get closer to realizing the vision of discipleship and ministry which Christ and the apostles point us to. So let us continue to challenge one another, and ask the hard questions about what we believe, and why we are doing things in a particular way.

He bids us build each other up;
And, gathered into one,
To our high calling's glorious hope,
We hand in hand go on. (Charles Wesley)[13]

Very good.

8

Of Presbyters and Priests –
An Anglican View

ANDREW TODD

As I understand my remit, I have been asked to provide an Anglican perspective on the question: What is a presbyter? Now I have to say at the outset that an Anglican probably would not start by answering or even asking that version of the question!

The designation of the ministry of word and sacrament as that of a presbyter has something of a low profile within Anglicanism. For example, the *Alternative Service Book 1980 (ASB)* rite for ordination to the priesthood has the title: 'The Ordination of Priests', with underneath in much smaller type and in brackets, 'also called Presbyters'.[1] This subtitle is little more than a passing reference, submerged by the overwhelming use of the word priest. It is clear, however, from a comparison of the *ASB* ordination service and that in *The Methodist Worship Book* that there is a great deal of overlap between the ministry expected by Anglicans of those they call priests, and that expected by Methodists of those they call presbyters.[2] My aim therefore will be to reflect on the Anglican question: What is a priest? But in doing this I hope that I will be considering a parallel question to that which is the focus of other chapters in this volume, within the same wider ecumenical debate about ministry.

Further, this will be a *reflection* on the Anglican version of the question, rather than a direct answer to it. For a direct answer to the question of what a priest is may conceal as much as it reveals. A single answer might well be partisan, and would almost certainly fail to reflect the nuances of the continuing debate about priesthood in the Church of England and the Anglican Communion. What I want to examine, therefore, is the change in the way Anglicans in the Church of England answered that question during the latter part of the twentieth century.

In brief, I want to consider the way in which understandings of priesthood have changed alongside changing notions of the relation of the Church to society, of apostolicity (seen in relation to mission) and of the Trinitarian nature of theology. Looking at these developments will enable us to look carefully at the different relationships envisaged in the Church of England between the ministry of the ordained and that of the laity. This may shed light on changing understandings of the interrelationship of the priesthood of Christ, of the Body of Christ and of those ordained to the ministry of word and sacrament.

The Demise of Christendom

To turn then to the relationship between church and society, I think it might be said that the Church of England has woken rather late to the demise of Christendom! The particular (and peculiar) relationship between the Church of England and the State, together with an attachment to the parish system, has meant that Anglicans in England have only begun comparatively recently to take serious notice of the fact that church and society are not identical and to tackle the implications of the discontinuity between the two. This has had a profound effect on thinking about ministry. As recently as 1986, the Board for Mission and Unity's publication, *The Priesthood of the Ordained Ministry*, referred quite unselfconsciously to 'community' without making any differentiation between the church community and the wider community. Thus for example:

> The special ministry is ordained to speak and act in the name of the whole community. It is also ordained to speak and act in the name of Christ to the community. Its authority and function are therefore not to be understood as simply delegated to it by the community.[3]

Consequently the ministry of the community is somewhat passive, while the ministry of the ordained is seen as within the community, and therefore within the Church. The movement of the priestly ministry of the whole Church is one of offering (in, with and through Christ) to God the Father. 'The Church's priestly offering embraces its prayers and liturgy, its love of neighbour and the proclamation of the Gospel in word and life.'[4] Alongside this, through the ministry of the ordained 'God makes present to his people the work of Jesus Christ, the mediator who brings humanity to God.' Within the community (which is both church and society) God's people encounter the priesthood of Christ, through the ministry of the ordained. In response to Christ's offering the people make their offering to God and so fulfil their priesthood.

Mission and the proclamation of the gospel are mentioned in the document, but there is little sense of the mission being carried out from the Church, by the Church. This is not surprising, because in an important sense the persistence of something like the notion of Christendom means that there is no 'outside the Church', or at least no *community* outside the Church. There is little sense of the Church exercising its priestly ministry (in and through Christ) within the wider community, as part of its ministry of reconciliation. And within the Church the major ministry seems to be that of the ordained to the Church, accompanied by, but distinct from, the response of the ministry of the Body – its offering to the Father.

Changing Notions of Apostolicity

It is difficult to say what it is that has begun to free the Church of England from this way of thinking. But one of the key signs that thought-patterns are changing is the emergence within Anglican theology of a different understanding of apostolicity. For much of the twentieth century debates about apostolicity have been driven by the desire for historical continuity. Robin Greenwood suggests that a number of factors led the Church of England to emphasize its credentials as a church which was in historical continuity with that of the first apostles. These factors included: the wrestling with the State for the control of the Church of England, which is an ongoing concern for English Anglicans; the reaction against the Papal Bull *Apostolicae Curae* of 1896 which declared Anglican orders to be null and void; and the general concern for the significance of the Church in a changing society.[5] In works such as Moberly's *Ministerial Priesthood*,[6] the place of the Church of England within a succession going back to the early Church was strongly stated. Further, this apostolic succession and the Church of England's membership of the catholic Church was seen as being guaranteed by the threefold orders of bishop, priest and deacon, and by the physical continuity of hands laid by bishops on those ordained. This sort of high-church thinking, while not the only point of view within Anglicanism, continued to dominate through much of the twentieth century, as was apparent (to the shame and regret of many Anglicans, including me) during the Anglican–Methodist conversations in the late 1960s and early 1970s.

However, more recently it is clear that a new and more dynamic understanding of the apostolic nature of the Church has been emerging. This is succinctly put in the report *Eucharistic Presidency: A Theological Statement by the House of Bishops of the General Synod*:

> The Church is *apostolic* in that it is grounded in, and summoned to be true to, the apostolic faith. It is also apostolic in that it is 'sent' ('apostled') in every generation: as Christ is sent by the Father, so the Church is sent by Christ. These two aspects of apostolicity are inseparable: faithfulness to apostolic teaching means the church can never forget its missionary calling, and authentic mission must be true to the apostolic faith.[7]

The message is clear. Resting on historical laurels is not enough; the Church needs to live in an apostolic way.

The impetus for such thinking is in large measure ecumenical dialogue. *Eucharistic Presidency* cites a number of such dialogues in its argument. And a further contribution to a theology of apostolicity comes from one such dialogue. The *Porvoo Common Statement* makes clear the role of the ordained in enabling the Church today to be apostolic by reaching out in mission.[8] The significance for Anglicans of the Porvoo Statement was that it enabled them in dialogue, for the first time, to look beyond questions about whether or not dialogue partners had a historic episcopacy, to questions about whether *episkopé* was exercised effectively in the Church today. As part of this thinking, we can see clarity in relation to the role of bishops: '[Bishops] *serve* the apostolicity, catholicity and unity of the Church's teaching, worship and sacramental life. They have responsibility for leadership in the Church's mission.'[9]

Represented here is a new understanding of apostolicity and of ministry. To be apostolic is not only to be in continuity with the first Christians, but also to live the apostolic faith by being apostles, by engaging in mission. This is the task of the whole Church (in all its constituent parts) and it is the ministry of all the baptized. The ordained do not act so much as a guarantee of apostolicity, but rather as those who enable the Church to be apostolic today. This turns earlier Anglican notions of ministry on their head. No longer is ordained ministry 'The Ministry', rather the primary exercise of the Church's ministry is by the laity, amongst whom the ordained act as *animateurs* – stimulating collaborative ministry.[10] The implications of this for priesthood will need to be drawn out in due course. But it is clear that this mission-centred understanding of how the Church can be apostolic signifies the recognition that the Church must carry the mission of God out into the wider community.

Trinitarian Theology

Another key dimension in the Church of England's shift of thinking about ministry has been the rediscovery of Trinitarian theology. Again it is difficult to establish cause and effect; but new understandings of the relationship between church and society and of apostolic witness go hand in hand with a move from a

Christologically driven theology to one in which consideration of all three Persons of the Trinity and of their relationship is significant for an understanding of ministry. The obvious example of such writing is Greenwood's book, already referred to, *Transforming Priesthood*. It is a complex theological shift to summarize. However, it seems to me that earlier theology looks backward to salvation brought about in the Christ-event, and at how people can continue to enter into that salvation through the life of the Church. I want to say that this is essentially *transactional*, about receiving salvation and responding to it.[11] And however hard proponents of this approach talk about the equality of ministries within the Body of Christ, it is clear that the ordained, in making salvation available through word and sacrament, have a much more active (and dominant) role than the rest of the Body.

The alternative, more recent, Trinitarian approach is essentially *relational*. Salvation is about entering into the community of being which is the life of the Trinity, and about participating in the outward movement of the life of the Triune God. The emphasis is therefore on the present and the future, on moving towards the *eschaton*, on sharing in the mission of God.[12] This is clearly in keeping with the emphases already considered within the emerging Anglican theology of ministry. It sits happily with the move from a historical understanding of apostolicity to one which focuses on being apostles. It also correlates with the acknowledgement that the Church is an instrument by which the Kingdom is realized in the world, rather than being the *locus* of the Kingdom.

But there are further dimensions to this thinking which expand the picture. The move from the transactional to the relational enables us to recognize the need for the Church to grow as a community of being (even if it is a pale shadow of the community of being which is the Trinity). Within that community, as the report *Eucharistic Presidency* makes clear, there will be 'a diversity of responsibilities and relationships', again reflecting in part the Trinity.[13] But this relational diversity will not imply superiority; nor should it be seen as implying a hierarchy, any more than the

Trinity is a hierarchy.[14] Such thinking contributes to an understanding of the collaborative ministry of the Body of Christ, in which the ordained exercise a particular ministry, serving the ministry of others.

Set Apart through Ordination?

I hope that the preceding paragraphs set out the background to the changing understanding of ministry within the Church of England. My intention was to show how thinking about ministry has been affected by a changing perception of the relationship between church and society, a corresponding shift in concepts of apostolicity and an underlying move to thinking in Trinitarian ways. The time has come to explore in greater depth the shift in the theology of priesthood in particular. My approach here will be to look at two different dimensions of this shift, mapping out earlier and later models of what it means to be priestly. The two dimensions will relate, on the one hand, to the question of the relationship of the priesthood of Christ, of the Church and of the ordained, and, on the other, to the celebration of the Eucharist. Finally, I will examine the extent to which the theory is reflected in practice, by looking at a vignette of the reality of Anglican ministry in this country.

There is agreement at every stage of the twentieth-century Anglican debate that priesthood may be attributed three ways. In the first place, priesthood belongs to Christ. According to Hebrews, Christ is the High Priest who mediates the New Covenant, through the sacrifice of himself, which once and for all brings forgiveness and the perfection of those who are sanctified. In one sense this is the totality of priesthood within Christianity, for, as Hebrews makes clear, the priesthood of Christ, who has entered into the heavenly sanctuary, has superseded that of the Old Covenant, which was exercised in earthly sanctuaries. Yet the Church has also understood the priesthood of Christ to be shared, so that priesthood is attributed secondly to the Church and thirdly to the ordained ministry.

Thus 1 Peter 2.9 is cited: 'You are a chosen race, a royal priesthood . . .' It is understood that by proclaiming the saving acts of God in Christ, the Church mediates Christ's sacrifice, making it available to the world. Further, the people offer 'spiritual sacrifices acceptable to God through Jesus Christ' (1 Pet. 2.5). Similarly, second- and third-century thinking is cited in support of a priestly theology of ordained ministry, particularly in connection with the role of the ordained at the Eucharist.[15]

If this threefold distribution of priesthood is agreed (albeit sometimes reluctantly), what has caused discussion and some dissension has been the relationship between the three. Anglican thinking in the earlier part of the twentieth century was driven once again by the need for a distinctive priesthood, which would form part of the credentials of the Church of England, establishing its place within the apostolic succession and the Catholic Church. It further sought to clarify the role of the ordained within the (church/society) community. Debate centred, for example, on how the priesthood of the Church and of the ordained ministry was *derived* from the priesthood of Christ. I have already cited some of the argument of the 1986 report, *The Priesthood of the Ordained Ministry*, which concluded of the ordained priesthood that:

> Its priesthood is not simply derived from the priestliness of the whole community. Rather, the common priesthood of the community and the special priesthood of the ordained ministry are both derived from the priesthood of Christ. Bishops and presbyters do not participate in a greater degree in the priesthood of Christ; they participate in a different way . . . Thus theirs is not a magnified form of the common priesthood; the difference is this, that their ministry is an appointed means through which Christ makes his priesthood present and effective to his people.[16]

It seems to me that this argument is problematic, fragmenting the unity of the Body of Christ. Further, the suggestion of parity between ordained and lay is not convincing, largely because there is no concept of an active exercise of priesthood by the

whole Body, no suggestion that it too is 'an appointed means
through which Christ makes his priesthood present and effective'
to the world. Later thinking is much more conscious of the relational nature of the Church, and of the mission imperative. The
1997 report, *Eucharistic Presidency*, discusses the problems of
metaphors such as derivation. It opts instead for the more
straightforward statement, drawn from the Anglican–Reformed
report, *God's Reign and Our Unity*:

> 'Priests' exercise their priestly ministry neither apart from the
> priesthood of the whole body, nor by derivation from the
> priesthood of the whole body, but by virtue of their participa-
> tion, in company with the whole body, in the priestly ministry
> of the risen Christ, and as leaders, examples and enablers for
> the priestly ministry of the whole body in virtue of the special
> calling and equipment given them in ordination.[17]

What we observe here is a shift from seeing the ordained priest as
set apart from the community of the Church, to seeing her or him
set apart *within* the Church.

Living the Eucharistic Life

In relation to the ordained priesthood and the celebration of the
Eucharist, the best way of portraying the difference between
earlier and later Anglican understandings is in terms of movement. The earlier-twentieth-century understanding of the
Eucharist may be seen as a movement inward and upward; the
later-twentieth-century vision is of a movement first of gathering
together and then of going out. The different understandings are
realized in church ordering and in the role and designation of the
ordained.

In the earlier understanding the altar/table is at the east end of
the church building, and is often raised up on a number of steps.
The ordained is designated as the 'celebrant' and stands physically between the people and the altar, symbolically between
them and God. That this is the symbolism is, incidentally,

confirmed by the minority low-church practice of celebrating at the north end of the table. Apart from being a misunderstanding of seventeenth-century practice, this removes the priest from the position of mediator between the people and God; a move which is in keeping with evangelical theology. The emphases in the majority tradition are, once again, Christological and trans-actional. The people come in and subsequently move forward to receive from God. What they receive is redemption in Christ. The ordained priest is the active participant in the service and (almost) the purveyor of Christ; the people are the passive respondents. The priest fulfils his (*sic!*) role of bringing the (church/society) community to God. This is a role of dual repre-sentation, of the people to God and of God to the community.[18]

In the more recent approach the altar/table is moved forward and often down several steps into the body of the church. The ordained is described as the 'president' and stands physically behind the altar, symbolically gathering the people around the table. (This piece of reordering, and the symbolism of gathering, are often rather hampered by the Anglican preoccupation with pews!) With this model, as Greenwood makes clear, the presi-dent is a *member* of the eucharistic community, as well as being the one who gathers it.[19] It is the whole church community which celebrates the Eucharist and lay participation (in roles other than that of presiding) is often more active than in earlier practice. The theology is relational; the Eucharist constitutes the com-munity as the Body of Christ. As *Eucharistic Presidency* puts it: 'The Eucharist is not an event for the autonomous believer, but the Church's participation in the Trinity's life, in which context the individual worshipper finds his or her place.'[20]

Further, the Eucharist is seen as enabling mission and there is a consciousness of the wider community in which the Church finds itself.

> With regard to the Church's apostolicity, here [in the Eucharist] the Church is directed back to the foundational saving history of Jesus Christ celebrated by the apostles, and discovers its calling as the body sent out into the world, to be

the royal priesthood in the context of daily life, anticipating the final consummation of the whole creation.[21]

In this model the concern is not just with coming to the Eucharist, but with living the eucharistic life. The ordained priest is here, not the controller of the process, but again the one who animates the community to celebrate and live the Eucharist. This is clearly a collaborative model of ministry, in which the ordained priest is a member of the *laos* but also has a distinctive role within it, amongst other diverse ministries. Again, we observe that she or he is set apart within, rather than apart from, the community. This raises a number of questions which have yet to be answered about ordination – for example, what is the difference between ordination and commissioning for lay ministries?

A Practical Theology?

I hope that the exploration of the two aspects of ordained priesthood in the Church of England have revealed a more three-dimensional picture of the changing Anglican answers to the question: What is a priest? What I would like to do finally is to point to ways in which the theoretical understandings are realized in practice. I am interested here in the extent to which the Church of England lives one or other model of ordained priesthood. I will suggest that we live, somewhat uncomfortably, with both, side by side.

The most significant way in which new understandings are becoming a reality is in developments within Anglican patterns of ministry. The stipendiary priests are no longer doing 'ministry' on their own. Their role is shared in the first place with a greater diversity of other ordained and accredited ministers. There are Non-Stipendiary Ministers (NSMs), who characteristically see their ministry in one of two ways. Most see themselves as auxiliary parish priests (exercising a ministry in the parish alongside work, or family life, or perhaps full-time having retired from secular employment). A much smaller number see their main ministry within their secular employment; these are known as MSEs. An indeterminate number will see their ministry as a combination of these two. There are also a growing number of Readers, lay people licensed to preach and teach, who may also exercise some kind of pastoral ministry.

More recently, these ministers have been joined by what are now known as Ordained Local Ministers (OLMs).[22] These are people whose vocation emerges, at least in theory, within the local church, as their gifts and calling are recognized by others, often during a period of development of lay ministry in that church. They are trained in part within that wider picture of parish development and the growth of a ministry team, or teams, amongst whom they will serve. After ordination (as deacon and then as priest) they are licensed to work collaboratively, under the supervision of the incumbent, only within the parish, or group of parishes, in which their vocation emerged and in which they will continue to live and minister. These ministers, most of all, indicate that the Church of England is moving towards the relational, mission-oriented, collaborative understanding of priesthood that has emerged in the last part of the twentieth century.

Yet the picture is not straightforward. Not all Church of England dioceses have OLMs, and some (although a decreasing number) are implacably opposed to them. Even in dioceses, like my own, which are committed to the OLM project, they enjoy a mixed reception amongst clergy and laity alike. Further, my suspicion is that collaborative ministry is still more talked about than done. And where it happens, it still tends to indicate greater concern for the development of 'churchy' ministry (ministry within the life of the church community), than with the ministry *of* the Church in the world.

More pessimistically, in some areas it seems that the Church of England has not got beyond the earlier model of the stipendiary priest being 'The Ministry' at all. For example, at ordinations and inductions we are still asking people if they will support the ordained in their ministry, rather than asking if they will share with them in it.[23] And it sometimes seems that what is driving the development of new ministries is *only* a shrinking budget and the need to respond to decreasing numbers of stipendiary clergy, rather than a *combination* of financial necessity and good theology!

The experience of MSEs is an interesting indicator of where the Church of England is. They, above all, are a sign that the Church is committed to moving outwards into the world, engaging in mission and encouraging all Christians in secular employment to think of themselves as ministers. But the small numbers of MSEs, and the lack of support which they all too often receive, suggest that we are not as committed to being apostolic as our espoused theology would have us believe. Their experience, together with that of the OLMs, leads me to conclude that the Church of England has indeed begun to practise ministry in a more relational way; we do have a sense of gathering together for ministry, of needing to engage in ministry as a church community. However, in terms of the other movement of contemporary eucharistic theology, that of going out in mission as the Body of Christ into the world, we have only just begun to draw together and encourage the individual ministries of the members of the Body of Christ.

9

What is a Deacon?

SUE JACKSON

Imagine the scene: the Formation in Ministry team takes to the floor for a quick foxtrot. The lay, presbyteral and diaconal members move in perfect harmony, gracefully complementing one another in their sequinned gowns of green, purple and royal blue. Well, I guess we can all dream (or is that 'suffer nightmares'?) . . .

My personal reflections began by pondering on dancing, Rublev's icon of the Trinity and also through a conversation with my quick foxtrot partner Ken Howcroft. We talked about the fairly traditional, processional model of the orders of ministry as they are found in many denominations, but noted that this model does not really fit with Methodist standing orders or candidating procedures. The perichoretic model best expresses my understanding of how presbyters and deacons relate – dynamically interconnected so that when you encounter one you meet a distinct emphasis of ministry but in such a way that you potentially meet each separate order. Deacon and presbyter seek to embody the same fundamental ministry but will tend to show a distinct, characteristic 'face' most in harmony with their call to one order or the other. And for the dance to be a creative, joyful one each partner needs to practise self-limitation. After stating this there is no point in being repetitious – what Ken Howcroft writes in the next chapter reflects my understanding.

However, such a presumption raises an important issue which I believe we have to address honestly as a church. In the past I have been foolish and naïve in assuming that the concept of 'equal and complementary' orders of ministry necessarily implies an image of partners dancing together in a circle, interweaving and enriching each other. I suspect there are many around who have either a Reformed view which can just about see the point of one (presbyteral) ministry, or a traditional threefold understanding where diaconal orders are contained within presbyteral ones. Thus, I am caught between a rock and a hard place, sensing that, as a church, we have not talked through the theology underpinning our standing orders. We need to share differing, implicit models, face disagreements and decide where that leads us.

So working with that picture of deacons and presbyters as dancing partners, we share in imaging the basic nature of ministry, focusing certain aspects quite specifically. This means I do not for a minute want to deny a presbyter's call to be a servant and, indeed, expect them to undertake their reconciling, overseeing role in a servant manner. But for ordination to make any sense to me, each of us should be focusing, in particular ways, different aspects of ministry. Surely attempting to focus everything ignores some fairly fundamental principles of optics and leads to total lack of clarity? Let us move completely beyond a strident, competitive 'Me too. I can do that' syndrome.

Presbyters and deacons are to refract the light of God going through all baptized people in different ways. The lens of each has a different focal point and so helps make different things clear. Also, each eye has a different position in the head, which means having two eyes gives richer vision and a fuller, deeper perception of the world (luckily I can use this picture at present without worrying how to include a third eye of bishops!). Modelling this as a circuit team just requires some clarity about what each focuses, confidence in oneself that both allows and celebrates the other person's ministry, and mutual respect.

Thus, primarily being positioned at the doorway rather than the pulpit, font or table and moving in and out from there does make a subtle but significant difference to my perception and, for example, the way I practise pastoral care. Deacons, members of congregations and people in the local community often speak of sensing this difference. Neither position is 'better' – simply

Too bad for folk like me who can't make do. Like one! Appalling example of not taking the partially sighted seriously different – and together they can help the whole church have a fuller vision of the world and our mission.

What is it that each of us is focusing? I would not dream of speaking for presbyters, but this is my understanding for deacons. *Diakonia* has been traditionally interpreted as lowly, humble service of the table-waiting and foot-washing kind which Jesus revolutionized by modelling and teaching himself, that to be the waiter was great. It also came to be seen as something that covered all ministry and thus should be typical of every Christian. *Diakonia* meant fairly mundane, routine, charitable work. As Jerome exclaimed, 'Must not a mere server of tables and of widows be insane to set himself up arrogantly over men through whose prayer the body and blood of Christ are made present?' Well, that puts me in my place. A slightly more heartening view was offered by Hiebert, who talked of *diakonia* as a voluntary, love-prompted service for the benefit of others.[1] It may involve prosaic, material table service but should go beyond such service.

Then more recently John Collins entered the scene with his seminal *Diakonia: Reinterpreting the Ancient Sources*[2] and became the hero of modern deacons. Through very detailed study he concludes that the '*diakonos*' family of words originally had three meanings: messenger, agent and attendant. Thus, the words apply to a person who takes things from one place to another; acts on behalf of and with the authority of God or Church; raises the dust by their hasty movement from one place to another; someone who provides things on call. Basically such a person is an agent of God's salvation, commissioned to bring a message, acting as interpreter and go-between: one who announces the Kingdom.

This understanding of the '*diakonos*' family of words certainly holds sway in current diaconal thinking. Even those who disagree with Collins have not been able to offer an empirically based counter-argument to date. Although welcoming much of his work, I have some reservations and would suggest that any simple adoption of his thesis is problematic for our Methodist tradition. Collins rejects the idea that all Christians are called into ministry (*diakonia*) by baptism, and that ordination is simply a setting apart for good order in the Church. Rather, ministry (*diakonia*) is a particular responsibility laid upon certain individuals alone. Secondly, *diakonia* equals the ministry of proclaiming God's salvation, maintaining the Church within the tradition, and encouraging its growth in peace and love – not loving service. I am unsure how this supports the argument for deacons as a group distinct from presbyters. I wholeheartedly accept the idea of deacon as ambassador, messenger and agent. But I worry that the role too easily becomes distorted if not seen in the light of things like Jesus' discussions over who is greatest or least, and the washing of feet that so upset and offended Peter. An unreflective stress on dignity and authority can lead to an ambassador who is highly respected and influential, lives in an embassy and jets around the world first class. Let us remember Jesus was an agent/messenger who radically redefined what authority, dignity, power and leadership meant.

And, before looking at what any new interpretation of *diakonia* might mean for deacons, it is important to remember one constant danger: our tendency to try and justify current practice by claiming legitimacy from text 'x'. This does little service to the integrity of either text or practice.

It is with this point in mind that I turn to Acts 6 and the question of what a deacon is and does – remembering that the term 'deacon' does not appear in the text. Exactly the same word is normally translated as *serving* at table or *ministry* of the word (an interesting example of the interpreter's values applying). And, whatever Stephen was martyred for, it was not for being in possession of a van full of perishable foodstuffs. This argues against a 'lowly table-waiting' understanding. But the text is certainly not straightforward if one is looking for a definition of 'deacon'. Stephen and Philip appear totally to disregard the given job description right from the start and act just like the Twelve. It seems to me that the early Church used the passage to legitimate deacons in a way that ignored what Stephen and Philip did and instead focused on the table-waiting and food-delivery tasks.

In the light of Collins's work and recent ecumenical diaconal thinking, an alternative interpretation might focus on the witnessing, teaching and evangelistic role of Stephen and Philip, and draw out the significance of the charitable acts. By this I mean that the acts of charity were aimed at bringing social and economic justice for vulnerable, marginalized people; forging links between different ethnic and cultural groups; connecting worship and congregation with service and the wider world; being involved in the same ministry activities of witness and proclamation concerning God's salvation as the Twelve, but in marginal contexts and with different people. The Twelve's position at the centre of the worshipping community contrasts with Stephen and Philip's role at the margins. They are therefore engaged in subversive, politically-charged, prophetic actions. The life and work of many deacons (and deaconesses) down the years has had this character. But the Church and deacons are always in danger of focusing simply on the individual charitable act rather than its subversive significance. And I wonder whether the temperament of some deacons leaves them poorly equipped to act at structural levels against injustice. Certainly, I need to address this in myself. I am aware, of course, that this reading of the text has as much to do with legitimating my preferred practice as someone else's alternative reading does.

Such an interpretation of Acts 6 is, however, in line with many official statements and documents about the diaconate that have appeared in recent years. There is much apparent similarity in response to 'What is a deacon?' among the various denominations and countries. I shall simply quote from two well-known responses that have informed subsequent papers.

The Hanover Report of the Anglican–Lutheran International Commission (1996) states:

> Christ is diakonos, servant, as the agent and image of the one who sent him, acting and forgiving with the Father's own power, mediating the Father's will to the world. Being diakonos does not mean that the roles of leader and servant are reversed or abolished, but rather that those who lead do so as servants, that is, as agents of God's salvation . . . A general

description of diaconal ministers can be given: Diaconal ministers are called to be agents of the church in interpreting and meeting needs, hopes and concerns within the church and society . . . Diaconal ministry typically not only seeks to mediate the service of the church to specific needs, but also to interpret those needs to the church. The 'go-between' role of diaconal ministry thus operates in both directions: from church to the needs, hopes and concerns of persons in and beyond the church; and from those needs, hopes and concerns to the church.[3]

And from the Windsor Statement on the Diaconate (1997):

> Within and across the denominations, the roles can and do differ. We increasingly perceive our role to be pioneering and prophetic, responding to needs, proactive in opportunity through commitment to mission and pastoral care within and beyond the church. Opening doors of opportunity, encouraging others to take risks, the contemporary diaconate acting in its capacity as 'agent of change', engages imaginatively and collaboratively with issues of justice, poverty, social and environmental concerns. We often find ourselves spanning boundaries, especially official ones of church and society.[4]

No doubt you can hear echoes here from the 1993 Faith and Order Committee report on the 'Methodist Diaconal Order'.[5] Do such official pronouncements fit with the self-understanding of deacons around our Connexion? Well, I asked a lot of my brothers and sisters what they thought a deacon is. 'Pastoral care' and 'mission/outreach' would sum up their views of diaconal work. Words such as go-between, bridge-builder, companion, enabler and co-ordinator commonly described the role. Being a member of a dispersed community was always mentioned (I shall return to this later). Certainly, the deacons differed in their emphasis within 'pastoral care' and 'mission/ outreach', the extent to which it was located within the congregation or wider local community, and how this understanding translated into practice. But the similarities were striking, from probationer to retired.

The first response I received was from a retired deacon and her description was constantly echoed: service of Christ, *in* and *through* the church (not 'to'), *with* fellow Christians (not 'to' or 'for'), *to* the world. Another wrote that a deacon is 'a publicly accountable servant of the church charged with modelling, encouraging and co-ordinating diakonia . . . Collaborative by nature, outward looking, growth orientated.' So, for example, pastoral care was typically seen as something involving building relationships and nurturing in order to help people discover and develop their own ministry in daily life.

What a deacon's ministry actually looks like is rightly plastic. In the words of our magazine this year, it is about being focused and flexible. Being focused allows and facilitates flexibility rather than muddled chaos or rigidity. And such plasticity is quite proper, indeed inevitable, if service is to be in response to need.

I want to qualify my next remark, but I feel that as a deacon I should primarily pay attention to my sacramental role in foot washing alongside presbyters concentrating on their sacramental role in Holy Communion. The first qualification: my focusing should only encourage and help others develop their particular gifts in service – not deny or impede. An interrelated, dancing image where each partner enriches the others is important here. And, secondly, I believe deacons should have a distinctive role in the Eucharist. Yet deacons are charged with constantly reminding and challenging the church over foot washing of the kind I described earlier. It appears that throughout history when there is an *over*-concentration on liturgical role this has always been at the expense of radical service and mission.

I cherish and rejoice in the role of table-layer and waiter, believing it needs to run through and link worship and service. I have a traditional view of the deacon's role in liturgy where, of course, the various symbolic elements need to be expressed in ways appropriate for the given context. This role is complementary to the presbyter's and has nothing to do with dispensations or competition: a dance that shows different partners moving together harmoniously. As an aside, I am conscious that sensitive thought needs to be given to the deacon's role in relation to lay people such as communion stewards or leaders of intercessory prayer. So, just a few ways in which involvement in Holy Communion expresses and informs the deacon's ministry:

• Preparing the table: through attention to mundane, practical, ordinary tasks the deacon helps people see all activities in their life as sacramental and potentially transformed by God. This is especially important for those who feel their lives are very limited, domestic or boring. At my ordination service the preacher said that presbyters were there to answer people's theological questions and deacons to point them to the local Citizens' Advice Bureau. After initially being upset and disconcerted by this piece of advice I have tried to ignore it, strongly believing that I am called to act as an interpreter and messenger of the gospel. As a deacon (rather than social worker or development officer) working on a deprived council estate my task was to be alert to God's presence and help people see the Kingdom being enacted in the Nursery Chimes group. Deacons too must 'mind the gap' Jane Leach writes about – often in boundary/edge places and involving the messy, menial, often dirty businesses associated with towels and basins.

• Having the role of carrying the paschal candle into church as the sign of Easter morning breaking into the darkness of Saturday night is another expression of the deacon's role. The action symbolizes how deacons are to act as messengers and go-betweens. Sharing in the darkness but keeping faith that it cannot overwhelm the flickering candle – witnessing to resurrection hope and helping people discover or maintain that hope even though 'society' has given up on their neighbourhood or life.

• Receiving the gifts and serving: deacons are about helping people discover and offer their gifts. Clearly, visibly integrating worship and service is vital but something many denominations fail to achieve (deacons too often are given either a liturgical function or work as a detached medical/ social officer). Such integration is necessary for several reasons: (a) to demonstrate the meaning and integrity of the service, (b) for the understanding, ownership and involvement of congregations, (c) for the recognition by society that what I may do is carried out on behalf of the Methodist Church rather than because Sue is a nice, kind person, (d) to help everyone recognize how their own worship and service are connected. The deacon's role in 'sending out' at the end of worship also relates to this. However, I would prefer to see it as 'going out alongside and, occasionally, slightly in advance of'.

- Incorporating intercessory prayers: deacons should take responsibility for ensuring needs within congregation, local community, wider society and world are included and addressed in relevant, appropriate and informed ways. This does not mean the deacon necessarily has to lead from the front. Instead they may co-ordinate and encourage those with most involvement or knowledge (in the fullest sense of 'knowing').

- Extending the table: deacons are engaged in the task of helping extend the table of fellowship and the messianic banquet to include those at, and beyond, the edges. One appropriate and very privileged way is through extended communion.✗

- The very obvious fact that deacons cannot 'do it all themselves' should be empowering for congregations; something to celebrate rather than be apologetic for. In relation to the Eucharist I am acknowledging the reality of my limitations, my need for others, and the fact that this is as God intends for all human beings – because it reflects God's Trinitarian nature and God's decision to choose self-limitation in relation to creation.

- Being unable to preside, and so perhaps having to prepare for and serve with someone who is a 'stranger' to the congregation with whom I work, can say important things about how power and leadership are to be exercised in the Church, if we are really serious about following Jesus' example and

+ This can be done
by any appointed person.

teaching. At least it can if an explanation is given about distinctive roles working in partnership, and I act with good
grace and eager willingness to share ministry with another.
Joint participation in liturgy should reflect a relational, interdependent quality of ministry between colleagues, where each
retains their distinctiveness. As we know, actions always
speak louder than words.

I think looking at our roles in Holy Communion is fruitful as a
way of understanding the distinctiveness of presbyter and
deacon and also the relationship between them.

Finally, I turn to membership of a religious order – a crucial
yet complex aspect of what it means to be a British Methodist
deacon. When Brian Beck spoke to the Methodist Diaconal
Order (MDO) at its Convocation a few years ago, he challenged
us to consider whether we were really a religious order or simply
a supportive fellowship. I do not want the MDO or Church to
get hung up on labels; after all, as far as I know the term
'religious order' was never actually applied to the Wesley
Deaconess Order by deaconesses themselves or others. The
terminology never mattered to them. What was deeply important was the nature, quality and purpose of their belonging
together. And that is what we need to reflect on as the MDO. It
is very obvious from conversations and reading their stories that
'something' to do with belonging to community has always been
vitally important in deacon(ess) self-understanding – for most
but not all members. I remember well the discussions at
Convocation during the early 1990s about whether we should be
an order of ministry and/or a religious order. The feeling of the
majority was that we were both, and that was the subsequent
decision of the Methodist Conference. Many were concerned
that being seen as an order of ministry could endanger our life as
a religious community. Yet some spoke of never really feeling
called to membership of a religious order. My impression then,
first as a greenhorn, and subsequently through conversation with
students, probationers, active and retired deacons is that the vast
majority strongly regard themselves as members of a mutually

supportive and accountable dispersed religious community, striving to follow a common rule of life and sharing in commitment to a ministry of servanthood. Deacons will tend to resist strongly any attempts to separate out the order of ministry and religious order dimensions, instinctively sensing the two are inextricably bound together and should remain so: integrating Mary and Martha, active and contemplative.

I acknowledge that in many denominations and places you can be a deacon without being a member of a religious order – but not a British Methodist deacon. I can envisage theoretically the possibility of being ordained to a diaconal order of ministry with a voluntary opt-in clause regarding a religious order open either solely to deacons or more widely. Personally I do not think I would be very happy with that. In passing, it appears from conversation that at least some of our sisters in the Caribbean very much regret having lost their sense of being a religious community upon becoming recognized as an order of ministry. I can also envisage having a religious order encompassing a variety of people and including some who were ordained deacons (like, say, the Franciscans). I prefer that model because it asserts that the foundation of ordained ministry should be religious community. But the question of how diffuse an order can be in its calling before it ceases really to be an order would need careful thought.

However, for the present discussion the fact remains that to be a British Methodist deacon means being a member of a religious order as well as being ordained to diaconal ministry. You very quickly pick up something of this 'belonging' through observing a group of deacons meeting up at some event! Always mentioned but hard to describe, I would like to use the words of some deacons, picked at random:

- An active deacon: 'It is about ties that don't bind but rather form a very supportive net.'
- A newly 'retired' deacon: 'Being a member, surrounded by others with a common purpose and commitment, has given me the courage to be more myself than I had ever been

previously . . . It helps in developing our own spirituality, which is what we do because of what we say we believe.'

- A newly ordained deacon: 'The essence of our being a religious order lies in the knowledge that everything I do, we do together. We are a geographically dispersed order, united by the "on the edge" nature of our ministry. Because of our unity, none of us stands alone.'

- A woman who remains active many years after retirement and who endured many hardships during her ministry: 'Belonging is part of our work . . . Costly, joyful, single minded commitment to our common calling has proved specific and exacting enough to create a profound sense of membership among those who share it and made possible a willingness and availability to go where needed.'

In common with all religious orders, our rule of life is itself a living thing that develops and changes with time and circumstances. Another similarity with other orders lies in each member having to take responsibility for interpreting a shared rule in ways appropriate for their own situation and follow it through by exercising self-discipline within a common discipline. At least, I have never yet known the Warden swoop in to make spot checks on unsuspecting individuals. The MDO rule of life is not different or more difficult to follow than that of any other Christian. It is not meant to be. Just as with ordination to an accountable representative ministry that is not better/different, so our rule is something anyone can live. The point is merely that we have made a public commitment to struggle to live and model it.

I was one of the first to ask hard questions and be critical of the Methodist Diaconal Order as an Order, but in looking at the subject of religious orders I came to think we might be able to use the term for the MDO. The three characteristics of obedience, poverty and chastity were certainly more *obviously* fulfilled by women in the Wesley Deaconess Order who were always single, very poor and often moved annually in appointments by the Warden. Nonetheless, the MDO today seems to show the characteristics Hill offers in his sociological model and we appear to have features of Aschenbrenner's active apostolic dynamic as outlined by George Lovell.[6] I guess most of us yearn to be able to claim Merton's description of the deacon as an active contemplative. That is what the MDO's holding together of order of ministry and religious order is striving after. As Sister Vera expressed it, 'Belonging is part of our work.'

Now if this belonging is simply to make us feel warm, cosy and loved (a sort of closed-off smugness for our own benefit) it should be rightly challenged. It is important that in Rublev's icon of the Trinity the circle remains open. Despite constant dangers towards holy huddles, I think the Order as a dispersed religious community does serve other purposes:

* Deacons working in what are commonly called 'presbyteral appointments' and experiencing frustration or pain as a result have said they are sustained by knowing they are part of a bigger group that is living out a diaconal calling.
* Deacons working in isolated, difficult and marginal places (which means they consequently experience marginalization themselves by church as well as society) say their ability to stay there is based on a strong sense of solidarity and mutual support where they are 'united by the "on the edge" nature of our ministry. Because of our unity, none of us stands alone.' Basil the Great asserted that Christian values of humility, obedience and love could be worked out only in the context of a *community* serving the needs of society. And many of us have found this to be true.
* It has been interesting when working on housing estates and with various groups quite hostile to organized religion that what has caught people's imagination and been attractive is the idea that I am part of a dispersed group that struggles to live with huge tension and differences, journey together as married/single, female/male, and be committed to mutual support. They respond to the idea that everyone is called to community despite assertions to the contrary in our individualistic society, and appreciate some people honestly

struggling (and often failing!) in their commitment to live it.

The 1993 Faith and Order report talks of deacons being signs of the presence and ministry of the servant Christ through 'the discipline, spirituality and commitment to community that is part of working out their personal vocation in the context of being a religious order'. Of course, community is not unique to the diaconate but building community to serve the needs of society should be always a distinct and important feature.

In working on diaconal theology, deacons around the world in the Diakonia Federation have produced this statement:

> Community is both gift and task, blessing and burden, a place of joy and a place of struggle and suffering [non-deacons who have observed us at Convocation or on our return will understand]. Community may make possible a corporate witness that is more powerful than the voice of the individuals . . . Community is both a way of life and a place to be . . . This sense of community exists even when members are separated by great distances. The bond that binds all communities is their spiritual life, their commitment to a lifelong call to service, which is sustained by the power of the Holy Spirit.[7]

And so I return to the place we began – with Rublev's icon of the Trinity – for an image of diaconal work and how deacons, presbyters and lay people link together in God's mission. Deacons, like Abraham, should be alert to strangers in need of hospitality. They are to help everyone remember that very ordinary tasks can be transformed by God and such acts of service in fact become moments of encounter with God. The three persons relate as equal, interdependent partners joined by loving mutual self-giving. And, very importantly, the circle remains open. God's nature is shown to be one of openness, incompleteness and chosen self-limitation – constantly inviting others to join the circle and enrich God's life. Therefore, the Methodist Church and its two orders of ministry must never exist for their own sakes and constantly need to be shaken out of their tendency to become closed, self-sufficient holy huddles.

What exactly service is will vary from deacon to deacon, place to place, and change over time. This plasticity is perfectly proper. But flexibility should not be simply the result of shortages on the stations or the preferences of presbyteral colleagues. Rather, the actual form a deacon's service takes should change in response to the needs of the world and the missionary tasks of the Church. Through the way they engage in activities deacons take seriously the idea that God's – and so the Church's – life must involve building community and connections. Belonging to a group that supports such action through mutual prayer and pastoral care gives deacons a foundation for this. Being human and fallible, deacons, together with everyone else, need to be challenged continually to keep the circle open, welcoming and outward looking.

There was something spk... about the Whole ~~deacons order~~ which, I fear, has gone. I think it is too early to evaluate the New order. I have my doubts about the whole business. In the 1960's John Wakefield (?) "our deacons are local spreaders, clan leaders, church stewards" etc. But a distinct order. This was forgotten k(?).

10

Ministerial Roles in Methodism[1]

KENNETH HOWCROFT

The starting point for Methodists is the *laos*, that inclusive community made up of those who recognize that they are the people of God and so act as a reminder and challenge to the rest of the human race who are in the 'image of God' (but do not recognize it) to become what God already considers them to be. In the New Testament the term is almost never used to denote 'lay people' as distinct from 'leaders' or other roles.[2] Instead it is used to describe the whole community of the Church.

Within that community, every member shares the Church's responsibility for offering worship and participating in mission. They fulfil this responsibility (or fail in it!) every moment of their lives, both when they are gathered in the church community and when they are dispersed in the world. Some members, however, are graced with special gifts or intense versions of common ones, or are simply seen to be the appropriate people to fulfil a particular need. They therefore take up particular roles within the life of the Church and on behalf of the Church in the world. Some do so as officers such as Class Leaders and Local Preachers, others as Lay Workers.[3] If such roles are at all long lasting they should receive appropriate levels of support, testing and authorization.

Some members, however, have felt themselves and have been judged by the Church to be called to exercise their particular skills and responsibilities in *an order of ministry* which also bears the marks of *a form of religious order*. Both of these involve a life-long commitment, the former to fulfil a particular role towards, within and on behalf of the Church, and the latter to undertake a common discipline and spirituality. At present

British Methodism has two such separate but complementary orders of ministry (diaconal and presbyteral) and is engaged in a debate about whether and how to create a third (episcopal).[4] Of the two current ones, the emphasis of the Methodist Diaconal Order has historically been on being a religious order (expressed through Convocation, the Rule of Life etc.), with the Order only recently being formally recognized as an order of ministry. It can be argued that the original emphasis of the body of Mr Wesley's preachers and helpers which eventually developed into the body of Methodist ministers (presbyters) was also on being a religious order. The inscription in the copy of the Large Minutes given to all who were received into full connexion said: 'As long as you freely consent to, and earnestly endeavour to walk by, these Rules, we shall rejoice to acknowledge you as a fellow-labourer.' Over the years, however, the emphasis has moved from this to that of being an order of ministry. There are now only residual traces of being a religious order, expressed in Ministerial Synods and the phrase in the new ordinal which follows the description of what presbyteral ministers are to do in God's name: 'These things are your common duty and delight. In them you are to watch over one another in love.'

Questions are immediately raised about how the orders of ministry relate to the whole community of the Church and to others who exercise roles of service and leadership within it. These matters were not clearly defined in the past because British Methodism only evolved gradually as a formal institution. Just as Christianity gradually developed from being a movement within Judaism to being a religious faith with institutions of its own so, somewhat analogously, Methodism developed from being a movement within the Church of England to being an institution or denomination on its own. Both processes occurred at different speeds and in different ways in different places. This tension between movement (or 'Society') and Church still influences the way that different ministerial roles are understood and exercised in Methodism today.[5] It is essentially encapsulated in the ambivalence with which Methodists emphasize the *ministry* of the *whole* people of God (sometimes borrowing language from elsewhere of '*every member ministry*') and yet insist on only thinking of the ordained when they use the term 'minister' (and even that often to the exclusion of those ordained deacon). Similarly, they have repeatedly insisted that the term *laos* or 'people' describes the whole community of the Church, yet in common parlance have used the term 'lay' to refer primarily to those who are not ordained. There are therefore two terms which they claim apply to the whole community, yet they equally insist on making one part of that community bear the weight of one, and another part the other.

Some people have attempted to solve this apparent dilemma by effectively proposing that the 'ordained' horn of it be abolished. Put starkly, such people ask not why this or that category of people should be ordained, but why anyone should be ordained at all. They almost invariably invoke the concept of the priesthood of all believers in their support. Yet the Faith and Order Committee has repeatedly stated that that doctrine does *not* mean (in Gordon Rupp's phrase) that Methodism must have 'an otiose ministry and an omnicompetent laity'. It is not really concerned with any *individual's* priesthood, but refers to the 'priesthood of the whole Christian community, derived from that community's sharing in the high priesthood of Christ himself'. It points to the whole community's declaration of its total obedience and offering of itself as a living sacrifice. Methodism has therefore not used the priesthood of all believers to say that anyone can do anything in the Church. Nor has it spoken of a special form of individual priesthood.[6] Nor again has it talked of a corporate priesthood or body of priests within the whole community of the Church. It has, though, talked in terms of a corporate body of ministers and, more recently, a corporate body of deacons.

What we have therefore are corporate bodies of ministers and deacons within the whole community of the Church. The ministry of the ordained and the ministry of the whole people of God are somehow inextricably linked. The one cannot be dissolved in favour of the other. Neither can be said to have priority over the other. The 1987 report of the Commission on the Two Sessions of Conference outlined two views of the relationship of ordained ministers to the whole Church:

> . . . To over-simplify, one view of ordained ministry would stress its historical continuity with the past, its representative character on behalf of the whole church, and the corporate responsibility of all ministers to watch over one another, to maintain fidelity to the gospel and to regulate their common life. This view stresses that ministers are ordained by those previously ordained. It also insists that the final decision not only on the admission or exclusion of ministers but also on the principles by which such decisions are to be taken, should lie with ministers. Another view insists that ordained ministry is one among many forms by which the church exercises the ministry of Christ, and that it is accountable to the whole church. This view would place emphasis upon lay participation in the ordination service and in decisions about admission and discipline, if ordained ministry is to be truly representative of the whole.[7]

That report prompts the reflection that over the years Methodism has been creating a synthesis out of these previously competing views. It was written before the Methodist Diaconal Order was formally recognized as an order of ministry. The two orders are not quite parallel in that it is a presbyter who presides at the ordination of deacons (with a deacon sharing in the laying-on of hands to symbolize continuity in the diaconate). Nevertheless, they are closely related and alike enough for a similar synthesis to be created in the case of deacons. So far as the ministry of the ordained (presbyters and deacons) and the ministry of the whole people of God are concerned, each requires the other: each legitimates and is legitimated by the other.

The nature of this relationship is addressed formally in Clause 4 of the Deed of Union in language which goes back in full to the signing of the Deed in 1932 and some parts beyond it to 1926, 1924 and 1908.[8] The relevant parts of Clause 4 state that

Christ's ministers in the church are stewards in the household of God and shepherds of his flock. Some are called and ordained to this sole occupation and have a principal and directing part in these great duties but they hold no priesthood differing in kind from that which is common to all the Lord's people and they have no exclusive title to the preaching of the gospel or the care of souls. These ministries are shared with them by others to whom also the Spirit divides his gifts severally as he wills . . . the Methodist Church holds the doctrine of the priesthood of all believers and consequently believes that no priesthood exists which belongs to a particular order or class of people, but in the exercise of its corporate life and worship special qualifications for the discharge of special duties are required and thus the principle of representative selection is recognized.

The 1974 statement on 'Ordination' extends this to say:

as a perpetual reminder of this calling and as a means of being obedient to it the Church sets aside men and women, specially called, in ordination. In their office the calling of the whole Church is focused and represented, and it is their responsibility as representative persons to lead the people to share with them in that calling. In this sense they are the sign of the presence and ministry of Christ in the Church, and through the Church to the world.[9]

als, the 1960 statement

Both the Deed of Union and the 1974 statement were written before the Methodist Diaconal Order was accepted as an order of ministry. They are therefore written with ministers (presbyters) in mind. Yet they are all that we have to draw on in order to gain a view of what it is to be ordained. Moreover, as we have noted above, the diaconal and presbyteral orders of ministry are not parallel but are similar and demonstrably closely related. With care it is therefore possible to explore the historical texts to gain an understanding of what it means to be ordained.

How, then, is the language of representative selection in these foundational texts to be understood? The Deed of Union is so keen to mark off particular types of understanding of priesthood or a priestly caste that it almost produces a cul-de-sac of negative definition which does not allow much to be said that is potentially creative. Yet even though the Deed does not want to say that the ordained are different from, and still less better than, other disciples in the whole people of God, it still wishes to emphasize that there is something distinctive and possibly even special about them. The Deed therefore proposes the concept of 'representative selection'. It is this concept that the 1974 statement seeks to develop in terms of 'representative persons' as it attempts to state an understanding of presbyteral ministry which would apply as much to those serving in sector appointments as it does to those appointed to circuits.[10] This seems to open up creative possibilities, but they are not followed through. The ordained are said to be representative, but it is not explained how. What precisely does 'representation' mean? Is the language of the Deed of Union a cul-de-sac, or can a creative way forward be found? *It can be very limited / fea*

The language of 'signs' becomes important here. A number of recent statements have talked of the ordained, and bishops in particular, being signs of the continuity of the Church in the gospel.[11] This can be developed to speak of them as being representative in the sense that they are signs of Christ and the Church in the world. Some of the background to this way of speaking can perhaps be found in the Bible. It can be argued that in some passages of the Bible there are descriptions of what might be termed 'prophetic signs'. Some of these can be seen as enacted metaphors or allegories: an example would be the story of Jonah and the gourd in Jonah 4.4ff. But sometimes the prophetic sign or action is seen to be performative, like the prophetic word. Both sign and word point to some previously unperceived or unacknowledged reality and to the consequences that will flow from it if particular action is not taken. By pointing to the reality they ensure that it is perceived, even if it is then ignored. In any event, people cannot avoid having to choose whether or not to take the necessary action. If they do not take it the predicted consequences will occur. Thus the prophetic sign or word heightens the possibility that people will recognize the reality and act properly to avoid the unfortunate or dangerous consequences. At the same time it heightens the chance of the consequences occurring, and so can be said to hasten them into being. Examples would be the story of Jeremiah and his pot in Jeremiah 19, and Jesus' action in the temple in Mark 11.15–19 (and parallels).

The prophetic sign therefore points to a particular reality and plays a part in its coming into being by representing it and, in a sense, becoming it.[12] Yet the reality is still 'other'. The prophetic sign is like a mirror image which stands, in some way, in the presence of the object or reality it reflects. Like mirrors in our everyday experience, however, the reflected image is not always an identical representation. It may be intensified or distorted. To use another picture, the sign may 'index' a complex reality, elements of the sign standing for, 'indexing', each part of the reality represented. Or the sign may be an 'icon', which is a direct representation of something. Examples here would be photographs and pictures. Yet a fundamental property of an icon is that it points to and is subservient to the thing it represents. It only has value as a means to an end. If it is valued as an end in itself it becomes an idol rather than an icon.[13] In this sense the ordained should become a transparent means through which Christ and his Church can be seen in the glory of God and the power of the Spirit.

Perhaps above all the ordained are iconic signs: objects possessing a perceptual ambiguity which, as we grapple with it, leads to an apprehension, clarification or reinterpretation not only of the thing to which it points but also of itself. Thus when we look at a cubist painting we might start by being confused. Then we might begin to see that it in some way represents a human face. Then we reinterpret the painting in the light of that intuition and see it more clearly. Then we begin to perceive, think about and understand the human face more clearly. In this sense, the ordained point to the reality of Christ and the Church in a way which enables people to perceive both that reality, and also the ordained themselves, more clearly.

For this to happen there has to be an agreement that the signs point to something. Signs are functions in negotiated systems of meaning. At one level the negotiation is between human beings. Theologically, however, God can be seen as an active party in the negotiation. The decision to ordain can therefore be seen as the negotiation amongst human beings and between God and human beings that those being ordained are to be iconic signs which act as mirrors of Christ and the Church. The actual ordination is then the empowering of the ordinands to become those signs.

A stimulus to further thinking here might be found in the report of the seventh series of the Joint Commission between the Roman Catholic Church and the World Methodist Council. This records a challenge in which 'Catholics ask Methodists whether they might not use sacramental language, such as has been used of the Church itself, of ordained ministry in the Church . . .'[14] If we analyse a mainstream theology of thanksgiving as it operates in respect of the Eucharist or Sacrament of the Lord's Supper we find that:

- the particular bread and wine that is used is not different from common forms of bread and wine but selected from them for particular purposes; it is received as from God, offered to God in thanksgiving and received from God again as the body and blood of Christ, transformed by the power of the Spirit into a sign of the real presence of Christ and an active means of Christ's grace in human experience[15]
- the particular people who gather together are not different from other human beings (since all are made in the image of God) but by gathering together they select themselves as those who wish to acknowledge God and themselves as God's people; they receive themselves as from God, offer themselves to God along with the bread and wine in thanksgiving and receive themselves from God again as the body of Christ, transformed by the power of the Spirit into a sign of the real presence of Christ. They thus become an active means of representing the world before God by sample and intercession and a means of embodying Christ's grace in the world.

It is fascinating to find here the concept of not being *different in kind* and the *principle of representative selection* for the discharge of special purposes. The language of the Deed of Union about ordination is obviously echoed in this. It may therefore be possible for that language to take on a new lease of life when seen in the context of a theology of thanksgiving. Thus

- those to be ordained are not *different in kind* from the whole community of the Church, but for the discharge of special purposes *the principle of representative selection is recognized*: the particular members of the community of the Church are received as from God, offered to God in thanksgiving and received from God again as successors to the apostles, transformed by the power of the Spirit into a sign of the real presence of Christ and an active means of Christ's grace in the Church and the world
- the whole community of the Church is not *different in kind* from other human institutions, but for the discharge of special purposes *the principle of representative (self-)selection is recognized*: the particular community which gathers together receives itself as from God, offers itself to God along with those to be ordained and receives itself from God again in succession to the Church throughout the ages, transformed by the power of the Spirit into a sign of the real presence of Christ and an active means of representing the world before God by sample and intercession and of embodying Christ's grace in the world.

Thus if the calling of the whole people of God (as outlined in the report 'Called to Love and Praise' and in the programme *Our Calling to Fulfil*[16]) is to be the Church in the sense of being the body of Christ in the world, presenting God-in-Christ to the world and the world through Christ to God, then the calling of those ordained in the Spirit can be said to be to represent God-in-Christ, Church and world by

- holding God-in-Christ constantly before the Church and the world

- holding the Church and the world constantly before God through Christ
- helping the Church and the world to see themselves and each other as God sees them
- being in the stead or acting on behalf of Christ and the Church.

It is worth noting in passing that those who are ordained therefore have to be able, knowledgeable, practical and spiritual theologians!

The calling of the ordained is therefore always to do with both what the person is and what she or he does. This means that we have to move beyond a sterile dichotomy between ontology and function. The concept of representation as outlined above helps us to do that. In particular representation relates to all of the following equally and wholly:

- who the ordained are, what they do and what they undergo
- their role
- their function
- their status.

To see in particular how the ordained represent the Church we must return to the four traditional marks of the Church.[17]

- They represent the Church in its calling to be *one* in that the various orders of ministry are collegial bodies visibly dedicated to seeking unity with God. They reflect in their own life both the oneness of God and the rich diversity of being and grace held together within it. They mirror the rich diversity of being and gifts found in the Church and the world and seek to connect and hold them together in the same oneness.
- They represent the Church in its calling to be *holy* in that they are set apart to spend time publicly as well as privately exploring ways of worship and spirituality and practising how to show the marks of Christ in their personal behaviour; and thereby prompt and enable others to do the same.

- They represent the Church in its calling to be *catholic* in that they are publicly deployed to embody links between God's people throughout history in this world and the next; to help create an authentic common life in belief and behaviour for the whole community of the Church both as it gathers and as it disperses; to be involved with the Church as it seeks the redemption of the whole world; and as part of those tasks to be openly committed to studying the tradition of Jesus, his apostles and their successors and to passing it on from the past to the future whilst re-embodying it in the present.
- They represent the Church in its calling to be *apostolic* in that they are publicly committed to facing the world in mission and witness in continuity with Jesus and his Church throughout the ages; to maintaining the tradition and continuity of being sent [i.e. stationed] as public agents of God's love in the world; and to undertaking particular acts of love in prayerful and practical service.

To see further in what sort of ways the various orders of ministry represent the whole community of the Church, it is instructive to look at the four major dynamics in the Church's life and purpose outlined in the programme *Our Calling* adopted by the 2000 Conference. Since British Methodism is considering whether to accept bishops into its life, in what follows there is an attempt to deal with the three orders of deacon, minister (presbyter) and bishop. It should be noted, however, that *as disciples all of those who are ordained participate individually in the life and work of the Church under those headings* alongside all other disciples. As leaders they do things with those whom they lead. Sometimes they do them on their behalf. They do not lead by managing from a distance, remote from the action on the front line and not engaging with those whom they lead in what they are doing. Beyond that, and only in that context do we find the distinctive emphases of the way in which the various orders of ministry represent the whole people of God under the headings of *Our Calling*.

The Roles of Ordained People in the Whole People of God: Shared and Distinctive

	Worship	Learning & Caring	Service	Evangelism
Headings from the process *Our Calling*	The Church exists to increase awareness of God's presence and to celebrate God's love	The Church exists to help people to grow & learn as Christians, through mutual support and care	The Church exists to be a good neighbour to people in need and to challenge injustice	The Church exists to make more followers of Jesus Christ
Deacon	Participates in worship and *leads* people to *link* the world to the sanctuary, and the sanctuary to the world	Participates in learning and caring and *leads* people to *extend* the nurturing and caring support of the church to the world	Participates in service, acts of compassion and acts of justice, and *connects* the church with the victims of injustice and the marginalized	Participates in evangelism and *embodies* the good news of Jesus in his or her action
Minister (Presbyter)	Participates in worship and *presides* at the word and the sacrament, at confirmations and at ordinations	Participates in learning and caring and *oversees* the church's teaching and pastoral work	Participates in service and *co-ordinates* church's acts of service	Participates in evangelism and *superintends* the saving of souls and forming of disciples
Bishop	Participates in worship, *presides* at the word, sacrament, confirmations and ordinations, and *provides* for the proper offering of worship in each place in her or his area of responsibility	Participates in learning and caring, *oversees* the church's teaching and pastoral work, and *teaches* the teachers and cares for the carers	Participates in service, *co-ordinates* the church's acts of service, and *speaks* and *acts* in the name of the church on behalf of the poor and oppressed	Participates in evangelism, *superintends* the saving of souls and forming of disciples, and *directs* the content of proclamation and the means of making disciples in his or her area of responsibility

The key words for deacons as they represent the whole people of God under the headings of *Our Calling* (as well as participating as disciples in the life and work of the Church under those headings) are therefore *leading, linking, extending, connecting* and *embodying*. The whole of Methodism can be said to bear the marks of a group of disciples in covenant with God and thereby with each other, with a life-long commitment to a common discipline and spirituality in offering worship and undertaking mission. But for Methodism to remember its heritage, to work out anew how to fulfil its calling in the present age, and to attract new disciples, those marks have to be publicly and formally re-presented. They have therefore been particularly focused within Methodism in the Wesley Deaconess Order out of which has now grown the *Methodist Diaconal Order* for both men and women. Within the Order people share in a common life and a collective responsibility, but as members of the Order they are ordained by prayer with the laying-on of hands under the authority of a resolution of the Conference. The 1995 Conference therefore reaffirmed that the Methodist Church recognizes and has received the diaconate from God as *an order of ministry*. As such its members are ordained by the Conference to undertake specific acts of service, liturgical and practical, within the community of the gathered church but particularly within the wider community on the church's behalf. Above all deacons focus the servant nature of Christ, and the Church, and of all Christian life, particularly with regard to the 'least of these' in and beyond the community of the Church[18].

It becomes increasingly important to identify a proper liturgical role for Methodist deacons. This must be distinct from that of ministers (presbyters), yet not undermine the proper roles and responsibilities of local preachers and worship leaders. At the same time it must not be something which has to occur in each and every act of worship and which can only be undertaken by a deacon, for there are still not many deacons active in the connexion.

Linking the world to the sanctuary could include:

- preparing and presenting candidates for baptism or confirmation
- bringing the elements of bread and wine to the communion table
- providing the people's concerns for the prayers of intercession.

In some traditions the deacon has also brought the special (Paschal) candle to be used in the Easter celebrations.

Linking the sanctuary to the world could include:

- leading those who have been baptized and confirmed to begin their service in the world
- taking the elements consecrated in the Communion service to those who are housebound or otherwise outside the gathered fellowship of church *Does well by 'Alms'?*
- taking alms to the needy and otherwise embodying the church's intercessory prayer in action.

The deacon might also be able to develop significant ways of symbolically taking lights lit from the Easter candle out into the world. *oh Lord — get down to earth*

The key words for the distinctive roles of ministers (presbyters) as they represent the whole people of God under the headings of *Our Calling* (as well as participating as disciples in the life and work of the Church under those headings) are *presiding, overseeing, co-ordinating, superintending.* Those ordained by the Conference as ministers to represent it in this way are not just the servants of the particular local communities to which they are sent, but also of the wider church as represented by the Conference itself. The continuity of the Christian Church throughout history is focused in the way that it ordains them as it has ordained a succession of others before. As such they remind the Church of its own history and development. They therefore accept a responsibility for remaining in touch with both the history of the Church and also the contemporary experience of the Church elsewhere in the world. They thereby represent and embody living links with the universal Church, in particular local churches, and so act as a living focus for the catholicity of the whole Church. They exercise this through visitation or 'looking people up for God', bringing wider pastoral and spiritual insights to bear on a particular situation whilst collaborating with local leaders who do so from local perspectives.

This pastoral care and guidance is offered to people as individuals, as groups and as communities in the wider world. The Church is visited not only when it is gathered in worship and fellowship, but also when it is dispersed in mission and witness. Those ordained by Conference to exercise pastoral responsibility in the form of oversight therefore have a particular concern for the apostolicity of the whole Church. Moreover since they are sent (or 'stationed') by the Conference to particular local situations they focus in themselves that general apostolicity.

The wider insights brought by those ordained by Conference to represent it are drawn from the contemporary experience of the universal Church, from the experiences of its successive generations throughout history, and from its historical traditions. This is true of deacons as well as ministers, but there is a special sense in which ministers focus the responsibility that the whole Church bears of drawing both old and new from the treasury of biblical, traditional and contemporary wisdom in order to gain understanding of particular situations, and thereby to respond to God in them. In order for that to happen in each particular context and generation, those strands of wisdom have to be passed on from the past to the future, even when they are not apparently relevant in the present. Those ordained by Conference as ministers (presbyters) focus the responsibility of the whole Church for renewing and handing on the tradition from the past to the present and on to the future. They exercise this role with and amongst the whole community of the Church in a particular place as the people gather before the Word and gather around the Table of the Lord. The former articulates and the latter enacts both the handing on and renewing of the tradition about what it is to experience God in Christ, and also the plunging of people into that experience.

Those ordained by Conference to exercise pastoral responsibility focus the holiness of the whole Church as they are ordained to the 'ministry of Word and Sacrament'. They bring universal perspectives to the ministry of the Word as they exercise that role in collaboration with others, such as local preachers, who bring particular or local insights to it. The same is true of the ministry of the Sacrament, for it is the whole community of the Church which 'celebrates the Eucharist' through the offering of thanksgiving. Presbyters have to preside at that celebration not because the *'ordained minister contributes to the Eucharist in his/her own person some essential element'* which makes the Eucharist into an *'offering of the people . . . specifically activated by the minister's presence'* or by some special priestly powers, but because presidency at the Eucharist is the point at which local and universal most intensely meet and where pastoral responsibility is most powerfully focused.[19]

The relationship between the diaconal and presbyteral orders of ministry starts to become important at this point. If the diaconal order focuses ministry as foot-washing service, what does the presbyteral order focus it as – manipulative mastery? Even if it occasionally seems like that in reality, it does not make for good theory or good practice. It has therefore become common to talk of presbyteral ministry in terms of 'leadership'. Yet that does not solve the problem. The biblical tradition has some uncomfortable things to say about power. Too often the exercising of power is left unrecognized and unanalysed in the life of the Church. Yet that means that it is not being offered to God and sanctified. Far from preventing abuse, the failure to name and discuss power is more likely to lead to it. It is not good enough for presbyters, for example, to hide behind a rhetoric that they are diaconal as much as deacons are simply because they are the 'servants of the servants of God'. The real challenge of the example of Christ to presbyters is not for them to cease to exercise their particular roles of *presiding, overseeing, co-ordinating, superintending* but for them to focus ministry and service in these roles in a way which seeks the good of the other person and of the Kingdom rather than their own. Thus a ministry of service for presbyters describes the way that they should undertake their distinctive roles. It is therefore different from the way that deacons exercise a ministry of service as their primary role. Similarly, the distinctive roles of ministers in leadership do not mean that deacons are excluded from leadership. There is an excellent summary of issues of power in the report 'Power in the Church' in the 1998 Conference Agenda pp. 451–3. In the 1997 Conference Report on 'Senior Officers of the Conference' there is a similarly good summary of leadership which develops (not before time!) ideas which had been raised in 'The Ministry of the People of God' Report in 1988.[20] It talks of the complex interaction of corporate and individual leadership, and of how all leadership is a form of service. It then states baldly that '*Ordained ministry is called into being to focus this insight for the whole Church.*' This would repay further explication, but it is hard to see how it cannot refer to diaconal as well as presbyteral ministry.

Both diaconal and presbyteral orders of ministry therefore represent leadership, but do so in different ways. The difference is shown by the part they each play in the function of pastoral responsibility or oversight. For Methodism, oversight is primarily found in the Conference. It is the whole community of the Church which shares in the common life of worship and mission and so exercises corporate oversight of it. In Methodism this oversight is embodied in the Conference which is made up of representatives of both those who have been 'ordained' and those who have not. By being part of the *laos*, realized in our structures by the fact that there is now a Diaconal Session of Conference, deacons share in the forming of that corporate oversight in the Conference. But they are not ordained to represent it.

Presbyters, on the other hand, are ordained to represent it. They exercise their pastoral responsibility as they represent and embody the oversight of the Conference in the particular places to which they are sent. This is irrespective of the type of appointment in which they are stationed (circuit, chaplaincy, connexional team, sector or other). The collegial body of presbyters has a mutual and interactive oversight in relation to both the gathering and dispersing church. That is why, contrary to common usage, it is <u>wrong</u> to define presbyters as being ordained to a ministry of word, sacrament and pastoral charge. In the language of Standing Orders, pastoral charge applies not to all presbyters but just to those who are appointed to circuits. It has a strong connotation of being 'in charge' of particular groups of members. This links with the phrase in the Deed of Union which states that those ordained by Conference (as presbyters) have '*a principal and directing part in these great duties*' which are the responsibility of the whole Church.

A better definition is therefore to say that all presbyters exercise pastoral responsibility as they represent and embody oversight. It is debatable whether describing that as 'pastoral' oversight is helpful or not. But it is important to note that because the Conference which they represent is made up of both lay and ordained, whereas they are by definition ordained, their exercise of oversight only comes to mature fruition when it is meshed again with those lay people and, where they are present, with those deacons who are participating in leadership in the various places to which the presbyters are sent.

It is here that we come to the problem of bishops. The key words which we used for their distinctive roles as they represent the whole people of God under the headings of *Our Calling* (as well as participating as disciples in the life and work of the Church under those headings) are *providing* for the proper offering of worship, *teaching* the teachers and *caring* for the carers, *speaking and acting in the name of the Church* on behalf of the poor and oppressed, *directing* the content of proclamation and the means of making disciples in their area of responsibility. There seems to be a huge overlap here with the role of presbyters. It may be that the ways in which bishops represent the whole people are a particular contextualization of the ways in which presbyters exercise oversight. The differentiating characteristic may just be that of geography, or regionality, and a collegial responsibility for the whole Church. This is the direction which the United Methodist Church has taken. Their bishops are consecrated and remain bishops for life, but they are not constituted as a separate order of ministry. They remain presbyters (or, as they would say, elders) consecrated to exercise collectively the assigned pastoral function of the 'general superintendency' of the whole Church, and to have responsibility for that ministry as individuals in particular contexts which are the area of one or two annual Conferences.[21]

This brings us to another conundrum about the interrelationship of the various orders of ministry. British Methodism has stated clearly that the presbyteral and diaconal order are separate and complementary. It is unclear whether this means that presbyteral orders do not contain the elements of diaconal orders. Our insistence that people from either order effectively have to re-candidate from scratch if they wish to offer for the other order would suggest that the one in no way contains the other. On the other hand our claim that we are ordaining presbyters in the Church catholic into what those traditions which have a threefold ministry would call priest/presbyter/ elder/minister would imply that presbyteral orders do contain diaconal (because that is the understanding in the threefold tradition). In those churches that have a threefold tradition this has usually been realized by successive ordinations as deacon, as priest/presbyter and, where appropriate, as bishop. That is the line that the United Methodist Church took when it had a 'transitional' diaconate which acted as a probationary period before ordination as an elder. Since 1996 it has no longer had a transitional diaconate, but a separate and complementary order of deacons. At the same time it has wished to maintain the idea that elder's orders contain deacon's orders. Since 1996 the UMC has therefore ordained deacons to the ministry of word and service, and its elders to the ministry of word, service, sacrament and order. If we went down the same route in Britain we would have to say that since our deacons do not have to be preachers they are ordained to the ministry of *word* (other than preaching) and *service*, whilst presbyters are ordained to the ministry of *word* (e.g. preaching, evangelism, apologetic, interpretation, speaking and acting prophetically), *sacrament* (e.g. in celebration and devotion, especially in baptism and Eucharist), *service* (e.g. pastoral care, acts of mercy and acts of justice) and *pastoral responsibility* (e.g. pastoral guidance, oversight, discipline and order).

It is perhaps worth flying a kite to see if we can get even further. The danger of talking of one order of ministry containing the elements of another is that it can easily be turned round into talk of one lesser or more specialized order issuing forth from a greater, fuller or more generalized one. This in turn suggests a processional view of the orders of ministry. On this view the college of bishops are the originators from whom the presbyters proceed. Deacons proceed from presbyters but also from bishops, in that they are often perceived as bishops' servants (as opposed to presbyters who are bishops' assistants). It is not surprising therefore to find that occasionally the tradition has talked of the orders of ministry in relation to a processional understanding of the Trinity: the bishop is like the Father; the priest/presbyter is like the Son who proceeds to incarnate the Father's presence and become the means of atonement being effected; and the deacon proceeds like the Spirit either from the bishop and the presbyter or from the bishop through the presbyter, as an ecclesiastical 'gopher'. — 'a *burrowing* American rodent'

But this is not the only model of the Trinity which is available. If Trinitarian analogies help at all, the *perichoretic* model is likely to be much more helpful. In this the three parties or persons dance round in a ring. They are interconnected and interpenetrated. They are each different, yet at the same time when you encounter one you encounter all three. If this has anything to say to the three orders of ministry, it implies that when you encounter one you meet a distinct emphasis of ministry but through that you potentially meet all three. The one taps into the dynamics of the other two, and can occasionally draw those dynamics into and through itself. Thus if there are no deacons or bishops around, a presbyter would have to fulfil diaconal and episcopal emphases by drawing them up from the depths of his or her being. Similarly, if a deacon finds himself or herself in a situation where there are no presbyters, he or she will have to draw up and present the presbyteral elements. In each case proper authorization will have to be given to regularize the situation. This will not make the deacon a presbyter, because in doing it he or she will be acting against the grain of the distinctive emphasis or identity of a deacon, but drawing from a dynamic of ordained life which is latent within him or her.

It is dangerous, of course, to push Trinitarian analogies too far, and they may even be inappropriate in the first place. If there is a point of contact, it is that just as concepts of the Trinity point to the internal dynamics of the deity so by analogy we might be able to catch a glimpse of the inner dynamics of what it is to be ordained. It is as important that there is one body of the ordained as that there are separate orders of ministry. The various orders of ministry are distinct but interdependent. They constitute and instantiate each other by their dynamic interactions with each other and with the world beyond them.

As we have seen, the main distinguishing mark of the ordained is that they represent the whole people of God in its call to discipleship and to be church. In a sense those who are ordained focus or represent what properly belongs to the whole Church. Yet there are dangers in this. Since ordained deacons, ministers (presbyters) and, potentially, bishops focus and represent in their various ways the common life and responsibilities of the whole Church there is a danger that they will be seen to be the body of Christ in the world more than those who are not ordained are perceived to be. Similarly, there is a danger that each individual will have to enact every part of that life and those responsibilities. Allied to a growing sense of individualism in our culture, this has tended to produce the ideal of the omnicompetent deacon, minister or, potentially, bishop up to which too many people have attempted to live. Yet the Methodist understanding is that it is the corporate bodies of those who are ordained who collectively focus those responsibilities between them. Those who are ordained therefore need to become aware of what it means to be part of a corporate body as well as to recognize their individual gifts, graces and skills. They also need to increase the ways in which they express to the whole people of God (gathered in Conference and elsewhere) their accountability for themselves as collective bodies of ordained people.

Ordained ministries (diaconal, presbyteral or episcopal) should not therefore be seen as the norm which defines all ministry, and all other ministries treated as if they were imitations of it. There is no implicit hierarchy in the relationship of the roles of the ordained to those of lay people. Lay people do not derive the form of their own ministries from that of the ordained, nor is the authority to minister delegated to them by the ordained. It is a travesty when lay people consider that their own service is a matter of being granted the privilege of helping the minister with his or her ministry rather than undertaking their own proper role in the work of the Church.

It is worth dwelling for a moment on the distinguishing marks of those lay people who exercise authorized ministerial roles in and on behalf of the Church. Earlier, we talked of people within the whole people of God who are seen as particularly gifted or as the appropriate people to fulfil a particular need. In fulfilling their discipleship they take up particular roles within the life of the Church and on behalf of the Church in the world, receiving appropriate levels of support, testing and authorization. Some do so as officers such as Class Leaders and Local Preachers, others as Lay Workers.[22] A group of Lay Workers from the Irish Conference[23] became animated when discussing whether it would diminish them in their current roles if the Conference of the Methodist Church in Ireland were to decide to ordain them immediately. The feeling was that they would be diminished in a number of ways. One would be in having to take on the general expectations and corporate role of representation inherent in belonging to an order of ministry, whereas they felt called as Lay Workers to a number of specific tasks. Another would be in having to take on a life-long commitment to a corporate discipline and mutual support and accountability inherent in belonging to a collegial body which has some of the marks of a religious order. They felt called as individuals to specific tasks limited by time and context. This might lead to a career for life in particular areas of work, but without a public life-long commitment to it.

What the Lay Workers did consider to be important was that

in some formal way, the Church (locally and connexionally) *recognized* the particular nature of their gift and their calling, *released* them to exercise it and *provided some resources* to sustain them in it. In addition some felt that it was important that they were publicly *authorized* to act on behalf of the Church, but others (e.g. those working in predominately Catholic areas of Ireland) thought that this would be detrimental.

Every member of the Church is, of course, a representative of the Church. Those who voluntarily undertake unauthorized ministries, and find that they are accepted by the Church in doing so, start to gain an additional seal of approval by that acceptance. Authorized ministries have a definite seal of approval. Yet there is still a clear distinction between those who exercise authorized lay ministries and those who are ordained. The difference is connected with the fact that those who are ordained belong to an order of ministry which also bears some of the marks of being a religious order. As we have repeatedly shown above, the complexity of ministerial roles in Methodism means that those who are ordained (deacons, ministers or bishops) must exercise their roles both amongst and with the whole people of God. This complementarity of roles is particularly important when developments in different forms of ordained ministry are being matched by the growth in number and forms of ministerial roles exercised by those who are not ordained. As the exercising of ministerial roles (in the general sense) by lay people is increasingly encouraged and officially recognized, both they and the particular roles of the ordained will increasingly have to be clarified.

The Ministry of the Presbyter

Philip Luscombe and Esther Shreeve

'Remember your call': Leslie Griffiths concludes his chapter with the words of the Methodist Service for the 'Ordination of Presbyters, usually called Ministers'. He seeks to recall the Methodist Church from its preoccupation with the day-to-day, the fashionable and the theories of the moment back to a set of older, perhaps eternal, values which have been half-learned by people who cry out in their need, but, he suggests, forgotten by the official representatives of the Church. Certainly a sense of threat and dis-ease is discerned by other contributors. Several ask whose task it is to address our question. Should we look to the official position of the Church expressed through the voice or vote of the Methodist Conference, or to the theology of the Church universal of which Methodism is a part? Or should we hold in mind the longing of those – both within and without the Church – who seek services, ministry, which the Church can no longer provide?

The individual chapters can be allowed to speak for themselves, but some broader themes are also raised. At the original consultation at Wesley House, discussion continued after the papers had been given, over the meal tables and late into the evening. Clearly here were topics which were of passionate importance and which engaged the imagination and concern of all involved.

The themes of this final chapter all arise out of our consultation. The individual issues listed here sparked the passion of those who took part. The most obvious gap is that there is no systematic attempt to build from the biblical witness or from a

theology of the Church to a theology of ministry. The contributors deal with immediate concerns as they see them. 'Called to
Love and Praise', the British Methodist Church's considered
statement on the nature of the Christian Church, provides a firm
base for future work. For many years now individual Methodist
Churches and the World Methodist Council have been engaged
in dialogue with ecumenical partners, resulting in many agreed
statements between Methodism and other churches. The continuing series of joint World Methodist Council–Roman Catholic
reports, for example, is little known but provides much rich
source material.[1] The 1974 Methodist Conference report on
'Ordination' was of crucial importance in firmly placing the
language of representation and focus at the centre of the Methodist understanding of ordained ministry, but it is a brief document, and much preoccupied with the introduction of 'sector'
ministry and other forms of diversity. A major task for the
Methodist Church in the next few years will be to attempt to
place ministry – lay and ordained – within the framework set out
in 'Called to Love and Praise'. The following issues will all need
to be addressed.

The Ministry of the Whole People of God

It seems unlikely that Methodism will find any convincing
answer to the question of what a presbyter is unless it also
addresses the question of the way in which God calls and equips
God's people in general for all the various forms of lay and
ordained ministry, and how these different forms of ministry are
related.

This book focuses on ordained ministry, and must therefore
deal with a series of hard issues concerning different understandings of ministry. If we understand ordained ministry as focusing
or representing the ministries of all Christians and the whole
Church then it is regrettable but not surprising that understandings of ordained ministry are at the forefront of the theological
concerns of most churches. Nonetheless, it would be unmethodist
indeed not to remark on the strangeness of this procedure. The

whole Church is the body of Christ, and with characteristic clarity Jürgen Moltmann reminds us of the mission of all Christians: 'The community of the baptized is the community of those who have been called. There are no differences here . . . Ordination, with its conferring of a particular charge, cannot enter into competition with baptism and cannot outdo it.'[2] The pioneering ecumenical document *Baptism, Eucharist and Ministry* made the same point 20 years ago:

> In a broken world God calls the whole of humanity to become God's people . . . All members [of the Church] are called to discover, with the help of the community, the gifts they have received and to use them for the building up of the Church and for the service of the world to which the Church is sent.

> Though the Churches are agreed in their general understanding of the calling of the people of God, they differ in their understanding of how the life of the Church is to be ordered . . . A common answer needs to be found to the following question: How, according to the will of God and under the guidance of the Holy Spirit, is the life of the Church to be understood and ordered, so that the Gospel may be spread and the community built up in love?[3]

That is not simply a question for those concerned with the ecumenical convergence of the churches, but should occupy each church as we seek to understand vocation and ministry in all their forms. Taken as a whole, the official British Methodist response to *Baptism, Eucharist and Ministry* was warmly affirming, but the comment on ordained ministry rings true: '[T]oo much space is devoted to the ordained ministry . . . greater attention to the ministry of the whole people of God might have revealed a convergence that would have facilitated discussion of the vexed questions relating to ordination.'[4] The 1988 Conference report on 'The Ministry of the People of God' attempted to redress the balance, but fundamental questions of the relation of lay and ordained ministries remain to be resolved.

The Education of God's People

Foundation training was introduced by the Methodist Church in 1999 to help recall the Church to a broader understanding of the varieties of ministry, and of the different vocations to which God calls God's people. All Christians are called, all have a vocation from God; some are called to positions of responsible leadership or ministry, recognized by the Church. We are used to speaking of education for ministry; we need to learn the language of Christian education for all, which has as its goals conversion, liberation and maturity. The love of God is forever at work redeeming the broken and sinful into a new creation. Christian education can never rest content with the transformation of the individual alone; rather, it seeks the conversion and maturing of the individual, the Church and society. Only within this wider context should we speak of education for ministry.[5] Christian education will form each Christian for the life of faith; many will also require specific training in order to fulfil their particular vocation. Thus talk of the ministry of the whole people of God needs to proceed alongside that of the formation of the baptized community through Christian living and education.[6] In practice different ministries require different training. The properly specialized training of the ordained (usually today together with a few lay people) must always clearly demonstrate that its purpose is to enable the education of the whole people of God.

The Place of Presbyters, Deacons and Bishops

It is not surprising that presbyters are often defined by what they are not. It is only a few years since Methodism reopened the Diaconal Order, and then took diaconal ministry formally into its system as a second order of ministry, parallel to the presbyterate. At the same time, the Methodist Diaconal Order was encouraged to reassert its particular identity as a religious order. The initial enthusiasm for a distinctive order of ministry remains strong, as Sue Jackson's chapter describes, but confusion and uncertainty also remain. Can enough Methodist circuits be brought to share the freedom and excitement of the vision of a distinctive diaconate so that deacons will not be forced into acting as presbyters in order to meet immediate needs? Can the distinctive vision be transmitted to a new generation of those considering a vocation to ordained ministry so that the Diaconal Order continues to be renewed and strengthened? Uncertainty is not confined to the Methodist Church; the General Synod of the Church of England has recently failed to adopt its own report on diaconal ministry, *For Such a Time as This*, which would have laid solid foundations for an Anglican permanent diaconate.[7]

It is not only the place of the diaconate that raises questions. The British Methodist Church is currently debating the possible introduction of episcopal orders. Oversight of some sort must always be exercised in any church, but since the death of John Wesley British Methodism has evolved a system of corporate oversight or episcopacy, under the supreme government of the Conference. Across the world, most Methodists have always lived with episcopal government, but despite the British Conference agreeing many years ago that there was no theological objection to the introduction of personal *episkopé* within the Church when the time was right, the topic continues to be controversial. The presbyterate in British Methodism is emerging from a period when it was self-evident that the word 'minister' stood for an ordained itinerant presbyter into a situation where the itinerant presbyters must co-exist alongside other forms of ordained ministry. There are now different possibilities for presbyteral ministry apart from life-long itinerancy, together with a renewed emphasis on the ministry of the whole people. It is hardly surprising that it has become both more difficult and more important to define the place of the presbyter.

A wider issue underlying this unease is of the relation of one form of ministry to another. Traditional Anglican and Catholic models inevitably assume a progression through the ordained orders of ministry, a model accentuated in the Catholic Church where a candidate traditionally proceeded through a succession of minor orders. Some will find this model helpful. Priests can never forget that whilst they represent – by the grace of God – the priesthood of Christ, they also hold within themselves the representation – again by God's grace – of the servanthood of Christ. Many others will find such a system irredeemably <u>hierarchical</u>. Those who *can* become bishops; most become priests; the least able or least favoured remain deacons. Methodists are deeply uneasy at any suggestion of a hierarchy within ministry, not least because they would wish to value lay ministry equally with that of the ordained.

Several recent discussions throw light on this subject. Stephen Croft's *Ministry in Three Dimensions* makes a strong case that the three traditional orders of deacon, presbyter and bishop each contain aspects of the other, whilst retaining a particular distinctiveness. Similarly recent Methodist reports such as *Episkopé and Episcopacy* helpfully spell out the distinction between the tasks of leadership that have to be performed, the way in which *episkopé* is currently exercised in the Church by individuals, groups, and – pre-eminently within Methodism – by the Conference, and the individual focusing of the symbol of *episkopé* in the person of a bishop. Ken Howcroft's chapter here makes a similar case. Nonetheless much work remains to be done. British Methodism currently keeps its presbyters and deacons entirely separate as orders of ministry. An understandable realism lies behind this approach. The office and work of deacons are already much misunderstood; if presbyters were also deacons it would be difficult to resist the impression that deacons were somehow unfulfilled or incomplete. Conversely, if Methodism does decide to introduce bishops, it is inconceivable that they will not also be presbyters. As Ken Howcroft points out, it is possible to argue from Methodist practice and history that bishops do not form a separate order of ministry, contrary to the almost universal experience of other episcopal churches. This leaves the Methodist Church with a difficult theological task: how can we best understand the different orders or focuses of ministry to be related?

Working as or Called to . . .

Methodism has never found it easy to define the particular calling of the ordained minister. The language of the Deed of Union reflects this unease. Over half of the short doctrinal clause is taken up with discussing ministry and the key phrases from 1932 remain at the centre of debate; they have been quoted already by several of the contributors to this book: 'Some are called and ordained to this sole occupation and have a principal and directing part in these great duties but they hold no priesthood differing in kind from that which is common to all the Lord's people . . .'

Grappling with these issues members of the consultation returned time and again to the necessarily public nature of ordained ministry: the deacon or presbyter stands in a public place, enters into the gap, in order to make public that there is more than this, that there are other dimensions, that God wills the Kingdom which is not-yet but will come.

On reflection, of course, it is obvious that many lay people are also called from time to time to exercise very public roles. Some would see the ordained as distinctive in that they uniquely hold together a ministry which is always public, publicly accountable and self-reflective. On the other hand it is clear that the Methodist Church today often employs lay people in similar roles, to which they may appropriately describe themselves as called. The report 'Episkopé and Episcopacy' helpfully analyses the role of lay and ordained leadership in the Church. More work is required here, but it does seem clear that presbyteral ministry necessarily involves a representation and focusing for the Church of what it is, and what Christ calls it to become. As Richard Clutterbuck suggests, this is pre-eminently demonstrated when the Eucharist is celebrated, but is at one with presidency at the church council and other essential tasks.

Many of the participants at the consultation wished to make a distinction between the place where each individual is called to serve by God – as presbyter, as deacon or to exercise another specific ministry – and the place where the Church needs them to operate, so that the Church can fulfil its own God-given calling. Many deacons, and not a few lay people, find themselves standing in the place of the presbyter. Thus individuals called to stand in one place, and to focus one aspect of the ministry of Christ, may find themselves expected by the Church to which they owe obedience to stand in a strange place, and to focus a different aspect of the ministry of Christ. It is vital for the individual (and for the Church) that both understand when the person is being asked to move beyond the role to which he or she is called and to stand somewhere else.

Any call to ministry is a call beyond our own capability to fulfil; in God's grace we are enabled to fulfil our calling. To be asked to take a further step beyond our calling in order to help meet the needs of the Church is a dangerous undertaking. Again, through grace, God does not fail God's people. For the sake of our own health though, and for the good of the Church, we do well to recognize and name those occasions when we need to minister in a different place from the one to which we were called. As a deacon remarked after competently working in a presbyteral role for several years: 'With God's help, I know that I can do it, but I am not called to it.' We need to understand the difference between *working as* and *being called to*.

Standing Together and under Authority

Standing in a particular place implies distinctive relationships with others. How do presbyters relate to the Church as a whole and to other presbyters? More than ever before the *Methodist Worship Book* ordination service stresses the corporate belonging of the presbyter to an order of presbyters. This claim is held in tension with society's expectations of individualism and personal fulfilment and with the rediscovery of the diversity of ministries to which the Church recognizes that the ordained may legitimately be called. A diversity of understandings of the presbyteral role is coupled with a variety of understandings of vocation, not to mention a welcome reaffirmation of the importance of vocations other than that of the ordained minister.

There may have been a time when all ministers were alike. Sometimes the old stationing procedures of the Methodist Church – remember Wesley's dream of monthly itinerancy – suggested that all ministers were round pegs to be fitted arbitrarily into round holes. Theological colleges used often to be referred to as vicar- or minister-factories, the production line churning out identical clones. No one would claim that this was the case now, and few would seriously wish to return to it, but can the Church cope with the individualism that has replaced it? Where does the individual presbyter stand in relation to the college of presbyters, his or her peers and colleagues? Or in relation to the expectations of society towards individual vocation and personal fulfilment? Or, most importantly, towards the Church of which he or she is only one part? The call of the presbyter is always a call to serve God's Church in public ministry and ministry under discipline.

Claiming a distinctive place to stand implies accepting the formal and informal relationships that bind the individual with his or her personal call to the shared vision of the college of presbyters and the corporate vision of the Church. In a church without bishops who stands in the place of 'guardian of the tradition'? The Methodist presbyter is a connexional person, called to bridge the gap between the local context and the catholic understanding of the faith of the Church. How are presbyters to be held accountable for the discharge of their call? Different branches of the Church, and different parts of Methodism have suggested different answers to this question. The presbyter is responsible to God, but also to God's Church. Is the accountability primarily to the whole Church, to local congregations, to the whole Methodist people as represented by Conference, or primarily to the college of presbyters of whom each individual is a part? As several chapters here suggest, Methodism has never found it easy to resolve this dilemma, and contemporary society where authority and dogma are both held at a discount is unlikely to be sympathetic to any call to discipline that is not accompanied by a compelling rationale.

Standing in the Gap

One of the themes which ran through the original consultation where these chapters were first discussed was provided by Jane Leach with her evocation of London Underground's clarion call: 'Mind the gap.' For her, presbyters are called to mind the gap between the now and the not-yet. Their task is self-consciously to embody the calling of all the baptized, who must struggle to bring about God's future. What they do is not different from the task of any Christian, but it is done in a self-conscious, articulate and public way. *Can you be called to that!*

In her chapter Jane uses the phrase in a very precise way but, as is often the way, the phrase took on a life of its own as our consultation progressed, and it could be very useful in future discussion. It helps to have the image in mind when we think about the Eucharist as the place where the present is porous to the future, and symbolically the minister of the Eucharist minds any number of gaps. The relationship which ministers have with the Church, individual churches and the world, and the tensions between Church and Kingdom seem also to have the potential to engage with a 'theology of the gap'. *If GcG a bit tiresome frankly.*

The Ministry of the Presbyter

As the presbyter presides at the Eucharist so she or he focuses the very centre of her or his calling. Such a ministry, of course, is only possible if lay people and deacons are called to stand somewhere else in *their* characteristic ministries. We might perhaps speak of the incomplete focusing of ministry by any of the ordained. Even the bishop is called to stand apart as a leader beyond a particular local community; the presbyter stands at the Lord's Table within the community, but linking the local church to the whole body of Christ; the deacon takes the door-keeping role between the local Christian community and the local community in all its variety. Each particular ministry is incomplete, representing only part of the ministry which Christ offers. Only when the *laos*, the whole people of God, gather together is there even the possibility that the Church can finally grasp the not-yet vision of the ministry of Christ represented through the various distinctive ministries of the Church.

Some good material here but ok for a Gordon Ruth or a Gordon Wakefield to make it interesting as Lumen with a bit of humour.

Some of it is too pompous.

And have you noticed? Money as who pays? is never mentioned —

I wonder when the old feelings of we become more and more complex. Or we do something like quietly creating a diaconal order as then they organize about it

Notes

Preface

1 George Guiver (ed.), *Priests in a People's Church*, London: SPCK, 2001.

Introduction

1 Edward Schillebeeckx, *Ministry: A Case for Change*, London: SCM Press, 1981, p. 207.
2 Methodist Church, *Our Calling*, Peterborough: Methodist Publishing House, 2000.

1. What is a Presbyter?

1 Deed of Union, clause 4. The current form of the Deed of Union is to be found in Volume 2 of *The Constitution, Practice and Discipline of the Methodist Church*, Peterborough: Methodist Publishing House, published annually.
2 Geoffrey Chaucer, *The Canterbury Tales*, translated by Neville Coghill, Harmondsworth: Penguin, 1977, pp. 16–17. Reproduced by permission of Penguin Books Ltd.
3 R. S. Thomas, *Collected Poems, 1945–1990*, London: J. M. Dent, 1993, pp. 42–3.
4 Thomas, *Collected Poems*, p. 54.
5 Anne Stevenson, *The Collected Poems 1955–1995*, Northumberland: Bloodaxe Books, 2000.

2. Mind the Gap

1 Lewis Carroll, *Alice through the Looking Glass*, London: Macmillan, 1872, ch. 6.
2 N. Young, *The Magicians of Manumanua*, University of California Press, 1872. Young argues that any identity is a matter of negotiation

between a commonly held myth and the personality of the individual assuming that role.

3 See Peter Berger and Thomas Luckmann, *The Social Construction of Reality*, Harmondsworth: Penguin, 1971, for a discussion of identity theory.

4 See Deed of Union, clause 4.

5 Jane Leach, 'Pastoral Theology as Attention', unpublished lecture, 1999.

6 Douglas J. Davies, *Studies in Pastoral Theology and Social Anthropology*, Birmingham: Birmingham University, 1986. See especially ch. 3 on 'Embodiment and Incarnation'.

7 Wolfhart Pannenberg, *Jesus – God and Man* (1964), British edition; London: SCM Press, 1968.

8 S. Anderson, 'The Story so far . . .', unpublished paper, 2001.

9 See H. R. Niebuhr, *Radical Monotheism and Western Culture*, New York: Harper, 1951.

10 Davies, *Studies in Pastoral Theology and Social Anthropology*, p. 21.

11 2 Corinthians 5.16–21.

12 T. S. Eliot, *Four Quartets*, 'The Dry Salvages', London: Faber, 1970, pp. 43–4.

13 Ephesians 3.18–19.

3. Where is the Minister?

1 See my article, 'Churches and Congregations', *Epworth Review*, 18/1 (1991).

2 From 'Called to Love and Praise', reprinted in *Statements and Reports of the Methodist Church on Faith and Order, Volume Two 1984–2000, Part One*, Peterborough: Methodist Publishing House, 2000, p. 51.

3 Gareth Jones, 'Foreword', in Jane Craske and Clive Marsh (eds), *Methodism and the Future*, London: Cassell, 1999.

4 David Clark, *Between Pulpit and Pew*, Cambridge: Cambridge University Press, 1982, pp. 77, 79.

5 Brian Beck, 'Some Reflections on Connexionalism', *Epworth Review*, 18/2 and 3 (1991).

6 Rupert Davies et al., *A History of the Methodist Church in Great Britain*, Volume One, London: Epworth Press, 1965, pp. 232, 233.

7 *Statements and Reports of the Methodist Church on Faith and Order, Volume Two 1984–2000, Part One*, p. 129.

8 *What Do You Think?* Peterborough: Methodist Publishing House, 1999, p. 34.

9 *What Do You Think?*, p. 23.

10 'Some Reflections on Connexionalism', *Epworth Review*, 18/2 (1991), p. 57.

11 Clive Marsh makes a similar point in 'The Practice of Theology in British Methodism', *Epworth Review*, 28/3 (2001), pp. 36ff.

12 See, for example, Nigel Collinson's Presidential Address on Conference in 1996 or Stephen Croft's comments in *Ministry in Three Dimensions*, London: Darton, Longman and Todd, 1999, pp. 11–12.

4. *Calling or Cop-out?*

1 *Methodist Conference Handbook 1974*, p. 81. This statement appeared as an editorial introduction to an article by Revd Ralph Fennell (then the first Secretary of the Committee for Ministry in the Sectors) entitled 'Sectors – A Sphere For Mission'.

2 Fennell, 'Sectors – A Sphere for Mission', p. 82.

3 'The Commission on the Church's Ministries in the Modern World', in Methodist Church, *The Methodist Conference Agenda 1968*, London: Methodist Conference Office, 1968, p. 504.

4 *Methodist Conference Agenda 1968*, p. 503.

5 *Methodist Conference Agenda 1977*, p. 331.

6 *Methodist Conference Agenda 1977*, pp. 326 and 328.

7 *Statements and Reports of the Methodist Church on Faith and Order, Volume Two 1984–2000*, p. 235.

8 *Statements and Reports of the Methodist Church on Faith and Order, Volume Two 1984–2000*, p.235.

9 There still remains a separate category of ministers in 'other appointments' – see Standing Order 740(2): 'ministers in other appointments includes full-time ministries exercised in any denominational or ecumenical body or agency other than one directly controlled by the Methodist Church' (*The Constitutional Practice and Discipline of the Methodist Church* [CPD], Peterborough: Methodist Publishing House, published annually).

10 The Standing Orders are reproduced in *CPD*.

11 Bernard E. Jones, 'A Theology of Sector Ministry?', *Epworth Review*, 4/1 (1975), p. 25.

12 'The Ordination of Presbyters, Usually Called Ministers', *The Methodist Worship Book*, Peterborough: Methodist Publishing House, 1999, p. 302.

13 'Report of the Working Party on Sector and Auxiliary Ministries', *Methodist Conference Agenda 1975*, p. 392.

14 *Statements and Reports of the Methodist Church on Faith and Order, Volume Two 1984–2000*, p. 261.

15 'Ordination in the Methodist Church' (1960), in *Statements and Reports of the Methodist Church on Faith and Order, Volume One 1933–1983*, Peterborough: Methodist Publishing House, revised edition, 2000, p. 101.

16 'Ordination' (1974), in *Statements and Reports of the Methodist Church on Faith and Order, Volume One 1933–1983*, revised edition, 2000, p. 111.

17 'Report of the Working Party on Sector and Auxiliary Ministries', *Methodist Conference Agenda 1975*, p. 402

18 Steven G. Mackie, *Patterns of Ministry – Theological Education in a Changing World*, London: Collins, 1969, p. 60.

19 'The Commission on the Church's Ministries in the Modern World', *Methodist Conference Agenda 1970*, p. 649.

20 David Chapman, 'Koinonia and Ordination', *Epworth Review*, 23/3 (1996), p. 80.

21 'The Report of the Joint Working Party appointed by the Division of Ministries and the Faith and Order Committee', *Methodist Conference Agenda 1977*, p. 326.

22 *Methodist Conference Agenda 1977*, p. 326.

23 *Methodist Conference Agenda 1968*, p. 504.

24 From an unpublished address entitled 'Ministry' delivered in the early 1970s.

25 'Towards a Theology of Ministry in Sectors', unpublished paper, 1993, para. 8.1.

26 'The Commission on the Church's Ministries in the Modern World', *Methodist Conference Agenda 1970*, p. 507.

27 'Ordination', in *Statements and Reports of the Methodist Church on Faith and Order, Volume One 1933–1983*, revised edition, 2000, p. 112.

28 *Methodist Conference Agenda 1997*, p. 586.

29 Jones, 'A Theology of Sector Ministry?', p. 26.

30 'The Report of the Joint Working Party', *Methodist Conference Agenda 1977*, p. 324. This was not the view of the authors of this report but a view that had been expressed to them.

31 'Report of the Working Party on Sector and Auxiliary Ministries', *Methodist Conference Agenda 1975*, p. 400.

32 'The Ministry of the People of God', in *Statements and Reports of the Methodist Church on Faith and Order, Volume Two 1984–2000*, p. 219.

33 See *CPD*, SO 510(1)(ii) and SO 610(1)(i).

34 Walker W. Lee and Arthur B. Shaw, *Patterns of Ministry in the Methodist Church*, London: The Methodist Church Home Mission Department, 1974, p. 22.

35 'The Ministry of the People of God', in *Statements and Reports of the Methodist Church on Faith and Order, Volume Two 1984–2000*, p. 221.

36 According to the list, there are also a further 35 ministers in 'other appointments'.

37 Of the 108 shown as being in sector appointments 37 are in chaplaincy
    appointments (hospital, prison, industrial and further education). They
    were excluded from the survey on the basis that, compared with the
    remainder, there is relatively little dispute today about the appropriate-
    ness of appointing presbyters to full-time chaplaincy posts.
38 See *CPD*, SO 743(1).
39 The point has also been made to me that it is not only sector ministers
    who are at risk of experiencing a sense of isolation. This can happen to
    any minister not in full-time circuit work – including supernumeraries
    and District Chairs.
40 *CPD*, SO 713(1).
41 See, for example, the comments made by Revd Malcolm Braddy, Chair
    of the Advisory Committee on Ministerial Appointments, quoted in
    'Flexible Patterns of Ministry', *Methodist Conference Agenda*, 1999,
    p. 253–4.
42 *Methodist Conference Agenda 1999*, p. 254.
43 From his Presidential address to the Ministerial Session of the 1959
    Methodist Conference, recorded in George Thompson Brake, *Policy
    and Politics in British Methodism 1932–1982*, London: B. Edsall & Co.
    Ltd, 1984, p. 299.
44 'Called to Love and Praise' (1999), in *Statements and Reports of the
    Methodist Church on Faith and Order, Volume Two, 1984–2000*, p. 6.

5. Priests and Prophets but not Servants

 1 See especially the three statements of 1993, 1995 and 1997 in
    *Statements and Reports of the Methodist Church on Faith and Order:
    Volume Two 1984–2000*, pp. 291–346.
 2 'Ordination' (1974), in *Statements and Reports of the Methodist
    Church on Faith and Order: Volume One 1933–1983*, revised edition,
    2000, pp. 108–19.
 3 *The Methodist Worship Book*, Peterborough: Methodist Publishing
    House, 1999, pp. 298–312, see esp. pp. 302 and 308, and also p. 297.
 4 '. . . (I)n strictly orthodox terms, Christocentrism is already theo-
    centrism . . .What we need is a shift from a bad Christocentrism to a
    good one', in S. T. Davis (ed.), *Encountering Jesus: A Debate on
    Christology*, Atlanta: John Knox Press, 1988, p. 28. Cobb was writing
    in the context of a dialogue with John Hick, but he could well have had
    some of the recent writing on the Trinity in mind, in which
    Trinitarianism and Christocentrism are sometimes polarized as easily,
    and as mistakenly, as theocentrism and Christocentrism.
 5 Paul Avis, *The Church in the Theology of the Reformers*, London:
    Marshall, Morgan and Scott, 1981, p. 1.

6 Re-focusing, re-visioning and re-branding are contemporary terms. I do not think they are inappropriately used for what happened at the Reformation.

7 I.e. a spiritual realm and a worldly realm, though as Cameron notes, Luther also referred to God's kingdom being in the world, against the kingdom of the devil (Euan Cameron, *The European Reformation*, Oxford: Clarendon Press, 1991, p. 153). The kingdom can also, of course, in Luther refer to 'the Last Day'.

8 See, e.g., *Institutes* Book III, Chap. XX. 42, in the context of his exposition of the petitions of the Lord's Prayer, where the kingdom is understood as consisting of 'two parts: the first is, when God by the agency of his Spirit corrects all the depraved lusts of the flesh . . . and the second, when he brings all our thoughts into obedience to his authority'. In the same section, Calvin can also speak of the kingdom 'flourishing within us' even if the 'final completion' awaits 'the final advent of Christ' (John Calvin, *Institutes of the Christian Religion Volume Two*, London: James Clarke, 1957, pp. 189–90). These observations are not, of course, meant to downplay the political significance of Calvin's thought. He is simply not to be read through more modern spectacles.

9 'We are continually forgetting that the kingdom of God is *within* us' (letter to John Valton, cited in Kenneth J. Collins, *The Scripture Way of Salvation: The Heart of John Wesley's Theology*, Nashville: Abingdon Press, 1997, p. 164).

10 For accounts of this history see, e.g., Mark Chapman, 'The Kingdom of God and Ethics: From Ritschl to Liberation Theology', in R. S. Barbour (ed.), *The Kingdom of God and Human Society*, Edinburgh: T. & T. Clark, 1991, pp. 140–63, or the editor's introductory essay in B. Chilton (ed.), *The Kingdom of God*, London: SPCK/ Philadelphia: Fortress, 1984, pp. 1–26, esp. pp. 4–8.

11 Though note Amanda Porterfield's comments on the Protestant background to the emergence of liberation theology via the work of Richard Shaull in the 1950s, in *The Transformation of American Religion*, New York: Oxford University Press, 2001, pp. 27–33.

12 I have long thought that the chairing of the Local Preachers' Meeting is one of the most significant jobs that a Superintendent undertakes in Methodism. It is at this point where this becomes true.

13 My caveats about worship are simply meant to indicate that Christian life and practice can too easily become collapsed into worship given that leading it will need to be a main part of a presbyter's life. But worship in that form will not, in fact, be what most Christians spend most of their time doing, and we forget this at our peril.

14 As a related, side issue: one of the things that interests me is the unevenness between baptism and Communion at this point. Methodism has

This tag always been so / christendom!

two sacraments, and both are normally administered by the presbyter, but there is a greater freedom about who can baptize, compared to who can preside at communion. In much of Methodism, despite 'the official version', it is undoubtedly true that only one sacrament is recognized. And I do not think the fault lines are simply to be ascribed to lingering Primitive and Wesleyan influences (though this would need checking out). Note, for example, cases in Methodism where a pulpit notice may still be given out to the effect that 'next Sunday morning's service will be a sacrament service'. This never means 'baptism'.

this is just the use of the term 'the sacrament' as on page 10 Para 2.

6. The Presbyter as President

1 Edward Schillebeeckx, *Ministry: A Case for Change*, London: SCM Press, 1981, p. 207.

2 John Zizioulas, *Being as Communion: Studies in Personhood and the Church*, Crestwood, NY: St Vladimir's Seminary Press. See especially ch. 6, 'Ministry and Communion', pp. 209–46.

3 The Baptist theologian Miroslav Volf has given a powerful critique of Zizioulas's ecclesiology in *In Our Likeness: The Church as the Image of the Trinity*, Grand Rapids, MI: Eerdmans, 1998.

4 Paul McPartlan, *The Eucharist Makes the Church*, Edinburgh: T. & T. Clark, 1994.

5 Hans Küng, *Why Priests?*, London: Fontana, 1972, p. 73.

6 Küng, *Why Priests?*, p. 81.

7 Robin Greenwood, *Transforming Priesthood: A New Theology of Mission and Ministry*, London: SPCK, 1994.

8 Greenwood, *Transforming Priesthood*, p. 145.

9 In addition to *Ministry: A Case for Change*, criticized by some reviewers for making historical overgeneralizations, Schillebeeckx also produced *The Church with a Human Face: A New and Expanded Theology of Ministry*, London: SCM, 1985.

10 Bernard Cooke, *Ministry to Word and Sacraments: History and Theology*, Philadelphia: Fortress Press, 1976, pp. 538–41.

11 Interestingly, the valuable essay on Christian ministry by Stephen Croft, *Ministry in Three Dimensions: Ordination and Leadership in the Local Church*, London: Darton, Longman and Todd, 1999, pp. 126–31, has a passage which explores the relationship between presiding at the Eucharist and exercising presbyteral leadership. The argument is not developed very far, and suffers by being hedged by too many warnings about over-concentration on the Eucharist, but it could form a good point for dialogue between traditions.

12 Greenwood, *Transforming Priesthood*, p. 173.

13 Robert K. Greenleaf, *Servant Leadership: A Journey into the Nature of*

Legitimate Power and Greatness, New York: Paulist Press, 1977. This – and other work by the same author – has been published by a Roman Catholic press and is currently used as the basis of a diocesan Continuing Ministerial Education programme in the Church of England.

7. Collaborative Ministry

1 *Statements and Reports of the Methodist Church on Faith and Order, Volume Two, 1984–2000, Part One*, p. 47.
2 P. McIsaac, 'The Role of the Laity in the Church', in Terry Charlton (ed.), *Spirituality for Lay Christians*, Nairobi: Pauline Publications, 2000, p. 155.
3 Hannah Ward and Jennifer Wild, *Guard the Chaos*, London: Darton, Longman and Todd, 1995, p. 124.
4 *Statements and Reports of the Methodist Church on Faith and Order, Volume Two, 1984–2000, Part One*, p. 238.
5 *Statements and Reports of the Methodist Church on Faith and Order, Volume Two, 1984–2000, Part One*, p. 251.
6 *Over to You, Reports from Methodist Conference 2000*, Peterborough: Methodist Publishing House, 2000, p. 36.
7 *Statements and Reports of the Methodist Church on Faith and Order, Volume Two, 1984–2000, Part One*, p. 249.
8 *Statements and Reports of the Methodist Church on Faith and Order, Volume Two, 1984–2000, Part One*, p. 245.
9 *Pilgrim's Way*, Manchester: Methodist Church, Resourcing Mission Office, 2001.
10 *Statements and Reports of the Methodist Church on Faith and Order, Volume Two, 1984–2000, Part One*, p. 125.
11 *Statements and Reports of the Methodist Church on Faith and Order, Volume Two, 1984–2000, Part One*, p. 133.
12 *Statements and Reports of the Methodist Church on Faith and Order, Volume Two, 1984–2000, Part One*, p. 31. 'Authorizations to Preside at the Lord's Supper' (1996) states: 'It is not appropriate to talk about the "right" to preside. No-one has such a right. Those who preside are authorized to do that which, in themselves, they have no right to do.'
13 *Hymns and Psalms*, Peterborough: Methodist Publishing House, 1984, no. 753.

8. Of Presbyters and Priests

1 *ASB 1980*, Oxford: Oxford University Press, 1980, p. 351.
2 Cf. *ASB 1980*, pp. 356f. and *The Methodist Worship Book*, p. 302.
3 *The Priesthood of the Ordained Ministry*, London: BMU, 1986, p. 99.
4 *Priesthood*, p. 98.

5 See *Transforming Priesthood*, London: SPCK, 1994, ch. 1.
6 London, 1897.
7 *Eucharistic Presidency*, London: CHP, 1997, p. 21.
8 The statement was the outcome of conversations between the British and Irish Anglican Churches and the Nordic and Baltic Lutheran Churches, and was agreed in 1992.
9 *Together in Mission and Ministry*, London: CHP, 1993, p. 25. My italics.
10 Cf. *Transforming Priesthood*, pp. 57f.
11 Cf. *Eucharistic*, p. 19.
12 See, e.g., *Transforming Priesthood*, pp. 64–8.
13 *Eucharistic*, p. 22.
14 See *Eucharistic*, pp. 22f.
15 See, e.g., *Priesthood*, ch. 5.
16 *Priesthood*, p. 99.
17 *Eucharistic*, p. 30; Anglican–Reformed International Commission, *God's Reign and Our Unity*, London: SPCK, 1984.
18 See *Priesthood*, pp.100–101.
19 *Transforming Priesthood*, ch. 6.
20 *Eucharistic*, p. 37.
21 *Eucharistic*, p. 39.
22 They were previously known as Local Non-Stipendiary Ministers (LNSMs).
23 I await the new ordinal, which will accompany *Common Worship*, with interest!

9. What is a Deacon?

1 D. E. Hiebert, 'Behind the Word "Deacon": A New Testament Study', *Bibliotheca Sacra*, 140 (1983).
2 J. N. Collins, *Diakonia: Reinterpreting the Ancient Sources*, Oxford: Oxford University Press, 1990.
3 *The Diaconate as Ecumenical Opportunity: The Hanover Report of the Anglican–Lutheran International Commission*, 1996, Anglican Communion Publications, 1998.
4 *The Windsor Statement on the Diaconate*, UK Ecumenical Diaconal Consultation.
5 Reprinted in *Statements and Reports of the Methodist Church on Faith and Order, Volume Two, 1984–2000, Part One*, p. 291.
6 M. Hill, *The Religious Order*, London: Heinemann Educational, 1973; G. A. Aschenbrenner, 'Active and Monastic: Two Apostolic Lifestyles', review for *Religious*, 45:5 (1986); G. Lovell, *The Methodist Diaconal*

Order as a Religious Order: Some Issues for Consideration, privately published for the Methodist Diaconal Order, 1993.

7 *Diakonia's Diaconal Theology,* Diakonia Federation, 1998.

10. *Ministerial Roles in Methodism*

1 This is an extract from K. G. Howcroft, 'Church and Ministry: A Theological Framework', which appears with 'On Being Ordained and in Full Connexion', 'Ministerial and Diaconal Competence', and 'Vocational Discernment and Formation' by the same author in *Formation in Ministry Papers,* to be published in 2002.

2 See 'Called to Love and Praise', *Statements and Reports of the Methodist Church on Faith and Order, Volume Two, 1984–2000, Part One,* p. 47.

3 See the Division of Ministries report 'Lay Workers in the Church', *Methodist Conference Agenda 1995.*

4 Faith and Order Committee report, 'Episkopé and Episcopacy', *Methodist Conference Agenda 2000,* pp. 120–49. The Guidelines in the report were adopted and a further report is to be brought to the 2002 Conference in the light of consultation about the section of the report dealing with the ways in which the Guidelines may be embodied in Methodist practice in the future.

5 *Statements and Reports of the Methodist Church on Faith and Order, Volume Two, 1984–2000, Part One,* pp. 34–8.

6 In recent years very occasional reference to ministers (presbyters) as priests or as having a priestly role has appeared in Methodist documents. An example is in the Faith and Order Committee report 'The Methodist Diaconal Order' adopted by the 1993 Conference, *Statements and Reports of the Methodist Church on Faith and Order, Volume Two, 1984–2000, Part One,* p. 308: '. . . Diaconal ministry particularly focuses the servant ministry of Christ and the Church just as presbyteral ministry particularly focuses the priestly and prophetic ministry of Christ and the Church.' Two questions arise from this. First, why has the 'kingly' element of the triad 'prophet, priest, king' vanished? Is it part of a failure to acknowledge and deal with issues of power in leadership (see further the discussion of leadership later in this chapter)? Secondly, is the mention of the 'priestly' element an important development, an unconscious assimilation to the thinking of some other churches, or an aberration?

7 'Commission on the Two Sessions of Conference', *Methodist Conference Agenda 1987,* pp. 718–57.

8 The current form of the Deed of Union is to be found in Part 1, Volume

2 of *The Constitution, Practice and Discipline of the Methodist Church*, published annually.

9 'Ordination' (1974), in *Statements of the Methodist Church on Faith and Order 1933–1983*, revised edition, 2000, pp. 108–119.

10 For more about this particular issue see 'On Being Ordained and in Full Connexion'.

11 See for example the 'Porvoo Declaration' and related statements; the Church of England House of Bishops' statement on 'Apostolicity and Succession'; and 'Episkopé and Episcopacy'.

12 There is a longer discussion of semiotics and the language of signs in K. G. Howcroft, 'Church and Ministry: A Theological Framework'. For an introduction, see Umberto Eco, *Kant and the Platypus: Essays on Language and Cognition*, London: Secker and Warburg, 1998. All discussions of semiotics must refer back to the work of Charles S. Peirce in publications such as *Collected Papers 1934–48*, *Semiotica 1980*, *Writings 1982–3*, *Categorie 1992*.

13 Thus George Herbert wrote in his poem 'The Elixir': 'A man that looks on glass/On it may stay his eye;/Or if he pleaseth, through it pass/And then the heaven espy', in which the glass is that of a telescope. If you look at the telescope glass and only admire that, you make an idol of it. If you look at it and only admire your own reflection in it, you make an idol of yourself. If you look through it at the heavens and admire them and the God who made them, you treat it as an icon.

14 *Speaking the Truth in Love: Teaching Authority Among Catholics and Methodists*, Joint Commission between the Roman Catholic Church and the World Methodist Council, Lake Junaluska, NC: World Methodist Council, November 2000, para. 68.

15 As Charles Wesley put it in the hymn now to be found at no. 602 in *Hymns and Psalms*,'Effectual let the tokens prove/And made, by heavenly art,/Fit channels to convey thy love/To every faithful heart'.

16 Methodist Church, *Our Calling*, Peterborough: Methodist Publishing House, 2000, and *Statements and Reports of the Methodist Church on Faith and Order, Volume Two 1984–2000, Part One*, p. 51.

17 See 'Church and Ministry: A Theological Framework'.

18 'The Methodist Diaconal Order' (1993), pp. 291–314.

19 *Statements and Reports of the Methodist Church on Faith and Order, Volume Two, 1984–2000*, p. 47–51. The quotations are from the Methodist response to *Baptism, Eucharist and Ministry*.

20 'Senior Officers of the Conference' (1997), *Methodist Conference Agenda 1997*, pp. 155–64; 'The Ministry of the People of God' (1988), *Statements and Reports of the Methodist Church on Faith and Order, Volume Two, 1984–2000*, pp. 229–81.

21 The UMC is effectively a federal system of annual Conferences, each of which covers the area of a medium-sized state (in fact, some Con-

ferences cover the area of two small states, whereas some large states have more than one Conference in them). Every four years there is a General Conference of all the annual Conferences, both those in the USA and those overseas, the powers of which have been delegated to it by those Conferences. The annual Conference is the basic body in the system.

22 See the Division of Ministries report to the 1995 Conference *Lay Workers in the Church*.

23 Lay Workers' Conference, Methodist Church in Ireland, Belfast, September 2001.

The Ministry of the Presbyter

1 The series began with an introductory report to the 1971 Denver meeting of the World Methodist Council and has continued ever since, addressing such issues as the Eucharist, ministry and revelation. The latest report is *Speaking the Truth in Love: Teaching Authority Among Catholics and Methodists*, Joint Commission between the Roman Catholic Church and the World Methodist Council, November 2000. For more details, see David Butler, *Dying to be One*, London: SCM, 1996, pp. 131–40.

2 J. Moltmann, *The Church in the Power of the Spirit*, London: SCM Press, 1977, pp. 301, 308.

3 *Baptism, Eucharist and Ministry*, WCC: Geneva, 1982 (F&O paper no. 111).

4 *Statements and Reports of the Methodist Church on Faith and Order, Volume Two, 1984–2000, Part One*, p. 425.

5 See, e.g., Mark Wakelin's 2001 Fernley Hartley Lecture, 'On Becoming, Living and Knowing', unpublished.

6 Cf. *Our Calling*; 'Learning and Developing as the Whole People of God', *Methodist Conference Agenda 2001*, p. 295.

7 *For Such a Time as This*, London: Church House Publishing, 2001.

[handwritten note] The next project to look at. History. I have just written a 10,000 word) article on the Catholic/Methodist dialogue Now?